VENEERING

A COMPLETE COURSE

VENEERING
A COMPLETE COURSE

Ian Hosker

GUILD OF MASTER CRAFTSMAN PUBLICATIONS LTD

First published 1998 by
Guild of Master Craftsman Publications Ltd,
166 High Street, Lewes, East Sussex BN7 1XU

© Ian Hosker 1998

ISBN 1 86108 046 8

Photography by Anthony Bailey except Fig 2.5, by Ian Hosker
Illustrations by Simon Rodway

Designed by Ian Hunt Design

Typefaces: Baskerville and Syntax

Colour origination by Viscan Graphics (Singapore)

Printed in Great Britain at the University Press, Cambridge

CONTENTS

To Tony and
Joyce Stephenson

INTRODUCTION

This book is devoted to describing the materials, tools, equipment and techniques that have evolved to produce the craft of veneering. As with all skilled activities, the techniques described here will need to be adapted to take account of individual circumstances – one of the skills needed to be a good practitioner of any craft is 'problem-solving'. Of course, the basic skills need to be mastered first, and the aim of this book is to help you acquire, to improve, those skills. I hope it is successful in achieving that aim, and contributes to your enjoyment of working with wood in what is, after all, a highly creative medium.

Working with wood enjoys the reputation of being an especially satisfying activity and veneering offers a number of opportunities for creativity, from 'pictures in wood' (marquetry) to the effects of alternating grain directions in geometric patterns (parquetry). It can be practised independently of other woodworking activities, or as an integral part of other crafts, such as furniture making.

Veneering does not require investment in expensive machinery – simple presses can be home-made – and gives you the opportunity to work with woods that may be unavailable, inappropriate, or too expensive, in the solid form. Some varieties are too weak structurally to be used in the solid form, and the veneer is the only feasible way to use them. Because it is possible to buy a huge range of wood species in veneer form, each with its own characteristic colour and grain pattern (figure), the opportunities for colour and grain combinations are practically endless.

I do hope that this book contributes to your skill development and enjoyment of this very ancient craft.

HISTORY AND TERMINOLOGY

♦ DEVELOPMENT AND USES OF VENEER

♦ PRINCIPAL FURNITURE STYLES

♦ VENEERING TERMINOLOGY

DEVELOPMENT AND USES

It is worth devoting a little time and space to the traditions of veneering. While not concentrating on its history, a brief look at its development will, I hope, establish the tradition of veneering and inlay as a highly skilled and prized craft.

The belief that a veneered surface represents an inferior version of a solid wood construction still persists in some circles. However, one visit to a museum or stately home, with their very fine examples of veneered furniture, quickly demonstrates the exceptional quality of craftsmanship that has been, and still can be, achieved. While it is true that veneer can mask a multitude of sins as far as the quality of the underlying groundwork (the surface on which the veneer is laid) or techniques of construction are concerned, the very highest levels of skill in woodcrafts are often to be seen as well.

Historically, veneers have been employed for a variety of reasons, some associated directly with providing decoration, and others having as much to

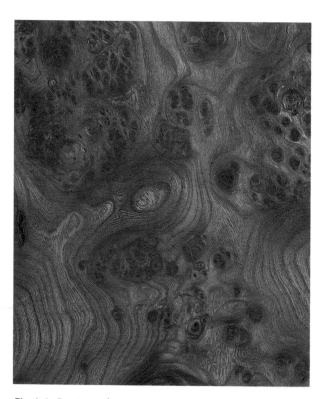

Fig 1.1 Burrs produce an exquisitely patterned figure, but the resultant timber is too weak structurally to use as solid wood.

do with making statements about the skill of the maker, or the power and wealth of the owner! After all, a cabinet richly decorated with marquetry represents many additional hours of work, and if rare and expensive materials have been used as well, the cost would have been enormous. Some woods have been, or are now, so rare or prohibitively expensive, that using them in veneer form is the only practicable way in which their decorative qualities can be exploited in a cost- or conservation-conscious way. Other woods are difficult to use in solid form because of their structural weakness. For example, burrs have such wild grain patterns, they are rendered very weak (*see* Fig 1.1). Burr veneers are cut from a large growth on the side of the tree. As a veneer applied to a much stronger constructional material, the decorative quality of such varieties can be gained without compromising the overall structural strength of the object concerned.

PRINCIPAL FURNITURE STYLES

One of the confusing aspects of studying furniture is the terminology associated with its history. For example, what is the difference between Age of Oak and Jacobean; William and Mary and the Walnut Period; Eighteenth century and Georgian; or Victorian and Arts and Crafts?

Figure 1.2 (*see* page 4) compares the historical periods associated with particular developments and styles in furniture crafts, as a guide to the nomenclature that readers will come across if they pursue further reading or research.

TERMINOLOGY

INTARSIA OR INLAY

This technique has a very old pedigree. It involves setting a solid wood pattern into a solid wood ground. Typically, the inlaid wood is of a contrasting colour to the groundwork. There are many fine examples of such work throughout Europe, dating back to late medieval times. The tradition of inlaying, however, goes well back into ancient times when the material used for inlays included precious metals and stones. An example of a fairly classic design is one in which holly, or a similar light wood, has been set into a very dark bog oak. This is genuine 'inlay', whereby pieces of wood are set, or laid into, a solid wood background. The modern usage of the word, as it is used in this book, applies the term to the principle of setting a contrasting veneer into an already veneered surface. This is a classic example of how language usage has changed over time. A totally incorrect application of the term is to use it to describe techniques such as marquetry and parquetry.

The term 'intarsia' has a long history, probably reaching Europe from the Far East. Intarsia forms the beginnings of what we now recognize as the general craft of veneering. However, intarsia also included the inlaying of gemstones and other precious minerals, and represented an expression of the wealth and power of the owner. Intarsia, therefore, can be regarded as a much earlier form of inlaying, using a wide range of decorative and highly prized materials.

To summarize, genuine inlay involves the setting in of one species of wood into a solid groundwork, though it is now frequently used to describe the sort of veneering work in which a contrasting species of veneer is set into a veneer ground. Sometimes, the technique may involve true inlaying, in that the background veneer is laid and then an area is cut out to set in the piece of contrasting veneer.

PARQUETRY AND MARQUETRY

If different species of wood veneer are used to create pictures or patterns, where the decorative effects are produced by contrasting colours and shapes, then we are moving into those areas of veneering called parquetry and marquetry. The difference between the two is in the decorative effect that is being created. Parquetry is a form of veneering where a repetitive pattern is created using pieces of veneer of geometric shape, such as squares, diamonds and triangles. Marquetry is the technique of creating pictures or shapes representative of recognizable objects – shells, vases

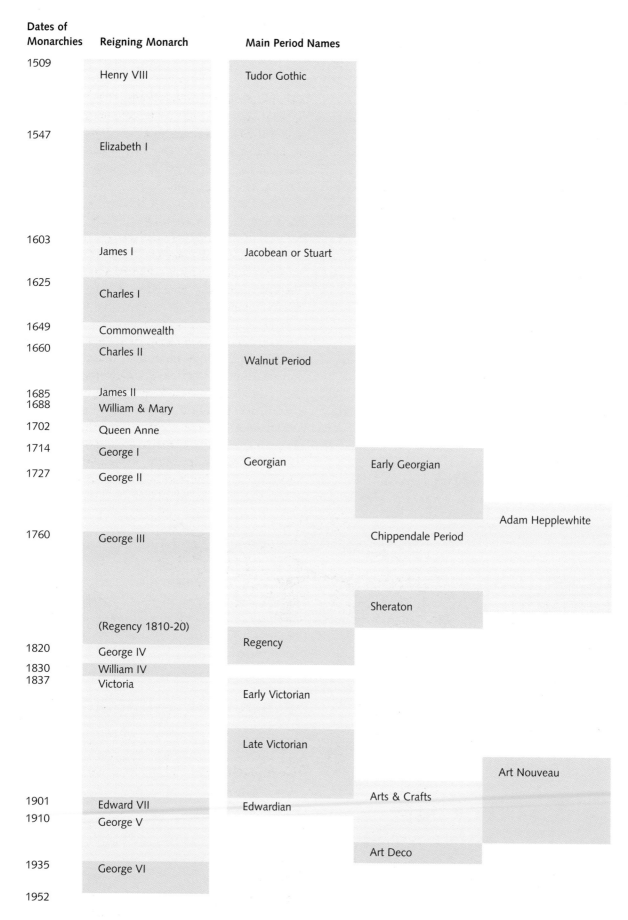

Dates of Monarchies	Reigning Monarch	Main Period Names		
1509	Henry VIII	Tudor Gothic		
1547	Elizabeth I			
1603	James I	Jacobean or Stuart		
1625	Charles I			
1649	Commonwealth			
1660	Charles II	Walnut Period		
1685	James II			
1688	William & Mary			
1702	Queen Anne			
1714	George I	Georgian	Early Georgian	
1727	George II			
1760	George III		Chippendale Period	Adam Hepplewhite
			Sheraton	
	(Regency 1810-20)	Regency		
1820	George IV			
1830	William IV			
1837	Victoria	Early Victorian		
		Late Victorian		
				Art Nouveau
1901	Edward VII	Edwardian	Arts & Crafts	
1910	George V			
			Art Deco	
1935	George VI			
1952				

Fig 1.2 Principal furniture styles.

4

and flowers are typical examples of marquetry on furniture – or are pictures in the sense of creating scenes. Landscapes and seascapes are frequently hung as pictures in their own right, as if they had been painted or drawn.

It seems appropriate to pay tribute to the skill of craftsmen of former ages. I cannot look at the quality of some old pieces of furniture, or other items of wood, without being staggered by the amount of work and skill they involve. That is not to say that these skills are not around today because they certainly are, in abundance, but it is rare that the levels of time required can be committed – it is generally too expensive – so these skills tend to be limited to very specialized areas of work, such as restoration.

By the same token, we are now used to a range and quality of tools that was not available to the craftsman of the Middle Ages, or even the eighteenth century. Modern veneers are also rather different. When you buy veneer today, you expect it to arrive in very thin sheets. Until machines capable of producing sheets of such uniformity

became available, veneers were cut by hand, with special saws. They were relatively thick, and not so uniform. Figure 1.3, a marquetry donkey, is included partly as a matter of curiosity, and partly because such machinery still exists and is used by some practitioners. While it is difficult to find and buy such equipment off-the-shelf, as it were, you may come across an example or wish to buy plans to make your own. The modern equivalent is the electric fretsaw (*see* Chapters 3 and 10), and what is curious is that those craftsmen I know who have used the machinery prefer the 'donkey' over any modern equivalent.

Both parquetry and marquetry can be taken to such extremes of complexity as to be breathtaking. Sometimes, materials other than wood may be used in the process. For example, Andre Charles Boulle (1642–1732) invented a form of marquetry during the late seventeenth century in which brass and tortoiseshell were used as the contrasting materials. There are also many fine Georgian and Regency examples which drip with intricate marquetry, depicting motifs inspired by classical designs.

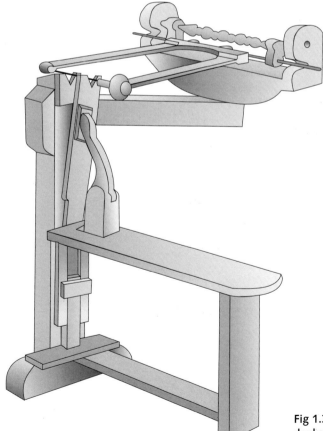

Fig 1.3 A marquetry donkey.

2

MATERIALS

♦ VENEERS

♦ GROUNDWORK

♦ ADHESIVES

♦ ABRASIVES

♦ POLISHES

VENEERS

Modern veneers are 'knife-cut'. That is to say, large logs of timber are securely held and thin slices are shaved off by the action of a reciprocating blade. Such blades move backwards and forwards to cut horizontally through a log. As veneers are cut, they are put into bundles of consecutive leaves. This makes it possible to supply matching leaves for use in such decorative effects as book-matching or quartering (*see* Chapter 7). This method enables very large sheets, or leaves, of veneer to be produced, with their thickness very accurately controlled.

Until the development of reliable circular saws after 1825, veneers were cut by hand using a large saw. This required two men to operate it and resembled an oversized bow saw. This technique resulted in much thicker veneers than knife-cut veneers – nearly $^1/_4$in (6mm) thick. From around 1830, huge circular saw blades were used and these could produce veneers closer to $^1/_{16}$–$^3/_{32}$in (approximately 1.5–2mm) thick. By 1914, the current methods of veneer production were in

universal use and veneers of extreme thinness – 0.03in (0.07mm) – were in general production.

Because of this, sawn veneers bear no resemblance to modern knife-cut veneers, which are

Fig 2.1 A comparison of knife and sawn veneers. The latter are essential for restoration work.

ready to use straight from the cutting machine. They were much thicker and often of uneven thickness so that they needed to be planed to a reasonably uniform thickness before they could be used (*see* Fig 2.1).

From a decorative point of view, veneering relies on two main qualities:

(a) contrasting colours; and

(b) interesting and/or dramatic figure (surface patterns and colour variations).

The techniques described later in this book will show you how such effects can be achieved. At this stage it is worth looking at several of the main decorative qualities of veneers, which is, after all, one of the justifications for their use.

CURL AND BUTT

Curl, a very dramatic veneer, (*see* Fig 2.2) is cut from the point in the trunk where it divides into two main boughs (*see* Fig 2.3). Since this occurs only at specific sites in the tree, a relatively small number of curl veneers are produced. This makes them expensive – and the cost tends to be in direct

proportion to the decorative quality. Butt veneer is cut from the opposite end of the trunk where the main roots divide. It resembles curl veneer, though the figure produced may be slightly wilder than curl.

Fig 2.2 Mahogany curl veneer.

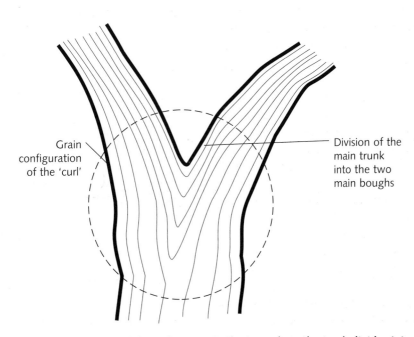

Grain configuration of the 'curl'

Division of the main trunk into the two main boughs

Fig 2.3 Curl veneers are produced from the point in the tree where the trunk divides into the main boughs.

BURR

This wild grain configuration (*see* Fig 2.4) is caused by the nature of the wood's growth. Burrs are those strange-looking growths that occur on the trunk of the tree (*see* Fig 2.5). They are often the result of some damage to that particular point. For a number of reasons an area of growth in the trunk (i.e. side branches or shoots) become damaged, perhaps through attack by insects or disease, causing a haphazard, localized growth, with many very small side shoots. The result is a bulbous protrusion from the trunk. The figure in the veneer reflects this haphazard growth. The circular spots are cross sections of the side shoots that make up the bulk of the growth. These veneers are particularly difficult to work with because of their brittleness. They frequently need patching prior to application because of damage. By their very nature, these veneers tend to be available only in small sizes, and are expensive because of their relative rarity.

Fig 2.5 An example of a burr.

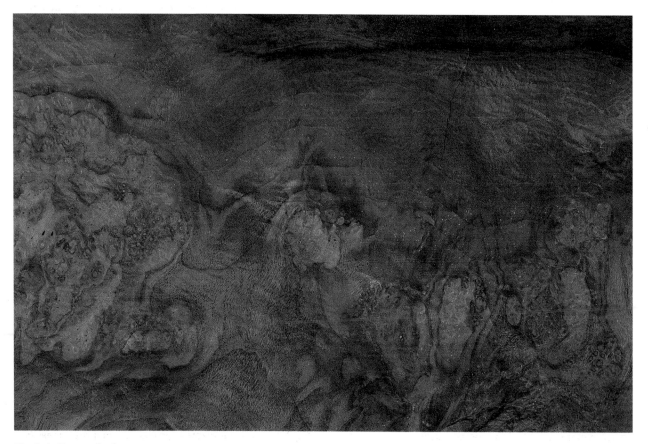

Fig 2.4 Burr walnut.

MOTTLED

This is not an official name, but it does adequately describe the very appealing quality of varying light and dark areas, that are at their most attractive when the veneer is polished (*see* Fig 2.6). These effects are caused by an undulating grain configuration. As the veneer is produced, the knife slices across the undulations so that the differing grain directions reflect the light in such a way as to produce areas of light and dark. These areas alternate as you view the work from different angles.

BIRD'S EYE MAPLE

This veneer is produced in a very different way in that the knife does not cut across the log in the usual way, but rather around its circumference (*see* Fig 2.7). As the knife will slice across side shoots, this produces lots of circles (annual rings), often with darker piths (the eyes), and it is these that create the decorative effect (*see* Fig 2.8).

Fig 2.6 This piece of satinwood exhibits a very marked mottled effect, produced by cutting the wood across wavy grain.

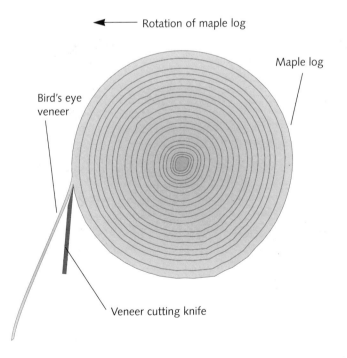

Fig 2.7 Rotary cutting of the log produces the characteristic figure of bird's eye maple.

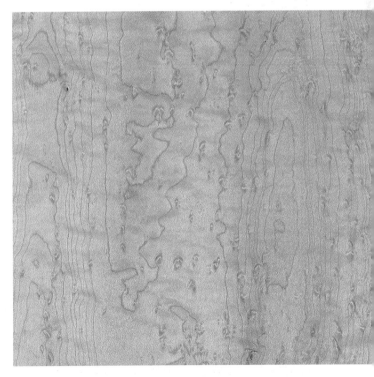

Fig 2.8 Bird's eye maple is produced when the veneer is rotary cut from the circumference of the log.

OYSTER VENEERS

These veneers, which are not at all common, are so called because their grain pattern resembles the surface of an oyster shell. They were very popular during the reign of Queen Anne (1702–1714), but today are used mainly in restoration or reproduction work. They are formed by cutting off transverse slices across narrow diameter logs (*see* Fig 2.9). Typical species used for oysters are laburnum, mulberry, lignum vitae and olive, however, there is no reason why any species could not be used. Their decorative effect is given by the variation in colour between the layers formed by annual rings.

Oysters are cut from the unseasoned log, approximately $\frac{1}{8}$in (3mm) thick, and need to be dried slowly and carefully to minimize the risk of distorting or splitting as they dry and shrink. If you cut your own, season them by stacking the oysters with waxed paper or plastic film (e.g. pieces cut from a plastic carrier bag) between each sheet. Store them in a cool place to slow down the moisture loss and reduce the build-up of tensions in the slices, and place a heavy weight on the stack to prevent distortion. The stacks should not be too high, as this will reduce the effect of the weight: 3–4in (75–100mm) is a good height.

Burying the leaves in silver sand would be ideal as this would slow down the seasoning even more.

The longer you can leave them to dry out the better – several months being essential. After removal from the sand, the oysters should be stored under the same conditions as other veneers. However, to prevent distortion, they should be weighted. Oysters must be made well in advance of any planned project, to allow for them drying out.

RESTORATION WORK

If your interests lie in restoration work, you will frequently come across items where the veneers are considerably thicker than those available from veneer manufacturers. The nature of the timber may also be different from that generally used today. For example, the characteristics of eighteenth-century mahogany are very different from those of modern mahogany because the varieties are different. For these reasons, most restorers will stockpile salvaged timber, some of which can be used to make veneers when required. You can make your own thicker veneers using a bandsaw, the maximum width of the veneer being determined by the machine's depth of cut.

MAKING VENEERS WITH A BANDSAW

A bandsaw is an ideal machine for making your own 'sawn' veneer. For most restoration purposes, you are unlikely to need veneers wider than 6in

Fig 2.9 Oysters are produced by cutting across narrow diameter logs, either at right angles to the length of the log or obliquely across it. Laburnum and holly are traditional timbers for this, but any narrow log can be used to create oysters.

(150mm). A lot of power is needed to cut through this thickness of wood with ease so the small, light duty machines are not suitable for this kind of work. The higher the power rating the machine has, the greater its depth of cut (i.e. the maximum thickness of wood it will cut). If you plan to buy a machine, then consider the following features. The general rule of thumb with all machinery is to buy the best machine your budget will allow, and for producing sawn veneers you need to be able to cut thick boards, so go for a machine that has a good depth of cut. You should consider 6in (150mm) an absolute minimum, but you should try and go for more because even though you may not need that extra depth of cut, the machine's motor will have a greater power rating and will then be under less strain with thinner materials. Another general rule is that the maximum width of blade is also linked to the maximum depth of cut. As described below, the width of the blade is an important consideration. In the case of most good quality, floor standing models suitable for a home workshop, the maximum blade width is in the order of $^3/_4$–1in (19–25mm), while an industrial quality machine will take a 2–2$^1/_2$in (5–60mm) blade.

The bandsaw blade needs to be the widest available for the machine, and the number of teeth per inch (TPI) should not be too great, as the thickness of material will be generating more resistance than the thinner material usually cut – there will be more heat and sawdust. The general rule is to use the widest blade with the coarsest cut that is available for your machine. The coarseness of the blade allows it to cut through the wood fairly quickly while its width will reduce the risk of blade 'wander', which will result in the veneer being of uneven thickness.

Wander can be caused by not setting up the blade properly, by insufficient tension in the blade, or by a knot or other hard area in the wood pushing the blade to one side. Narrow blades are more prone to wander because they twist more easily if deflected by a knot. Because a wide blade is supported by the wood behind the cutting edge it is less able to twist, and therefore less easy to deflect and less likely to wander.

The ideal blades for cutting veneers are skip tooth blades, in which the teeth are very widely spaced for faster cutting and easier sawdust clearance. They also generate less heat and so are less likely to scorch the wood.

Whatever blade is used, it is best to cut the veneers a little over-thick and then plane or sand them to the correct thickness. This has the added advantage of removing the machine marks.

Figure 2.10 shows how the bandsaw is set up to cut the veneer. Notice that a wooden fence has been attached to the standard fence of the machine. The purpose of this is to provide additional support to the timber as it is fed through the machine to ensure a consistent cut. A set square is used to ensure that the new fence is vertical and parallel with the blade.

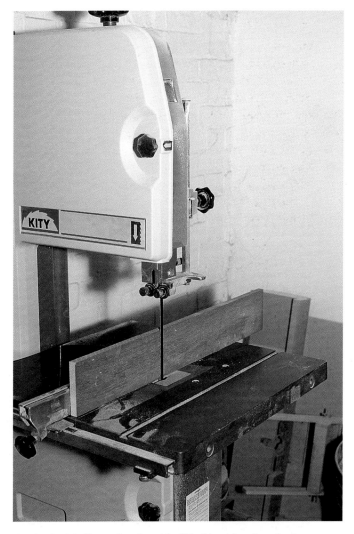

Fig 2.10 A tall wooden fence is fitted to a bandsaw's rip fence to enable accurate cutting of thicker veneers. The blade and wooden fence must be parallel.

BANDSAW METHOD

1 Carefully set the fence at a distance from the blade equal to the thickness of the veneer, ensuring that the fence is vertical and parallel to the blade. When measuring the distance between the fence and blade, it is important to take into account the set of the teeth. In Fig 2.11, the distance A is used, *not* B, which would make the veneer thinner than intended (it would be undersized by a distance equal to the set of the blade).

2 Plane the face of the wood used to make the veneer flat and true, and hold this hard against the fence.

3 Slowly feed the wood into the blade, allowing it to cut at its own speed. The sharper the blade the better. Do not force the wood into the blade as this will only encourage it to wander and create a very uneven cut. There is always the danger of the veneer becoming trapped between the blade and fence, so carefully remove the veneer once it has been severed from the main timber stock.

Entrapment can be avoided by carefully guiding the veneer away from behind the blade as it is cut.

4 If more veneers need to be cut, plane the exposed surface flat and true between cuts. This will help to ensure consistency in the thickness (*see* Fig 2.12).

MAKING VENEERS BY LAMINATION

If you do not have machinery, then it is possible to produce veneers of sufficient thickness by gluing two or more thinner veneers together. The veneers are glued together under pressure in a veneer press (*see* Chapter 3). Each layer, or lamina, has its grain direction at right angles to its adjacent lamina. (See Balancing and Counter Veneers in Chapter 5.)

This is not the ideal method for making thicker veneers, as it may be necessary to reduce the thickness after gluing into place, to make it lie flush with the surrounding surface. The risk here is that you will cut through the top lamina revealing the glue line and the lamina beneath, with its grain direction lying at right angles to the rest of the surface.

Fig 2.11 Calculating the thickness of veneer coming off the machine. The distance 'A' is the measurement to use. If distance 'B' is used, the veneer thickness will be undersized.

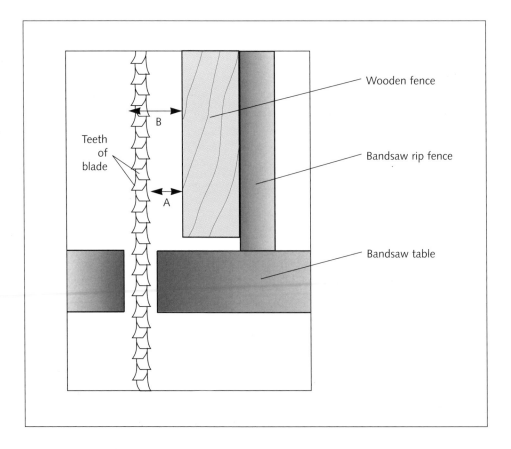

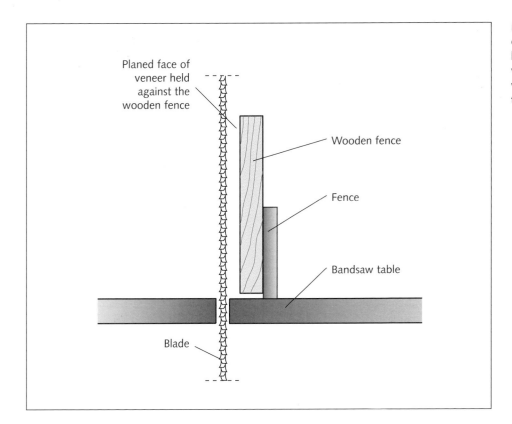

Planed face of
veneer held
against the
wooden fence

Wooden fence

Fence

Bandsaw table

Blade

Fig 2.12 The planed face
of the veneer stock must
be held tight against the
wooden fence to ensure a
veneer of uniform
thickness.

GROUNDWORK

Veneer needs to be laid onto a solid surface. This is
called the groundwork. Historically, groundwork
was solid wood, so for restoration work this will
need to be copied. However, there are some serious
disadvantages with solid wood groundwork (*see* page
14), and nowadays it is unusual to use it as the
manufactured boards available provide a very
reliable and stable base for veneers.

Veneer laid over plywood, or any other
manufactured board, is often regarded as a
combination of two inferior materials, but this is
unfair to both. As discussed in Chapter 1, there are
many fine examples of veneers, displaying the
highest level of skill and quality of craftsmanship,
and it is worth spending a moment to explain, in
general terms, the value of manufactured boards
such as ply, blockboard, medium density fibreboard
(MDF) and chipboard. These all offer a stable, flat
surface, and provided they are of good quality there
will be no blemishes to show through the veneer.
Their most notable quality, though, is that they do
not shrink or expand in width or thickness: it is this

shrinkage and expansion in solid wood that
provides so much work for furniture restorers!

SOLID WOOD GROUNDWORK

The use of manufactured boards as groundwork is
now so commonplace and taken for granted that
the role of solid wood as groundwork is rarely
considered. However, in restoration work it may be
necessary to replace solid wood groundwork. Also,
high quality reproduction or copy work will
frequently use contemporary methods, including
solid wood ground. In the mid-seventeenth century,
when veneering was becoming widely practised in
Britain, craftsmen used oak groundwork as this was
the predominant furniture making timber. The
problem with oak, though, is that as it shrinks, the
hard medullary rays (those flecks that are
characteristic of oak) do not, so they stand proud of
the surface and show through the veneer, creating
an uneven and bumpy surface. Pine makes a
suitable groundwork, provided it is not too knotty,
or the knots are cut out as described on page 16.
However, in very high quality work, it is not

unusual for mahogany to be used as the groundwork beneath highly decorative mahogany or walnut veneers. Mahogany makes good groundwork because of its mildness and stability.

If solid wood is to be used as the groundwork, it is important to take a few precautions to reduce the risk of problems later. Wood has a tendency to shrink or expand in its width and its thickness in response to changes in its moisture content. It does not shrink or expand in its length (i.e. along the direction of the wood fibres). However, it is a little more complicated than that because there can be a

differential in the amount of shrinkage or swelling at various points according to where the wood was taken from the tree, or because of variations in the direction of the wood fibres (i.e. grain direction). This then leads to rounding of the board, as shown in Fig 2.13. In addition, there may be surface defects, such as knots, that do not shrink or swell at all. As the groundwork shrinks it will leave these features standing proud of the surface.

All of these changes in the shape of the groundwork will have an effect on any veneer which is laid onto it. As the veneer becomes stressed, it may crack or show stress marks. Special techniques need to be adopted to minimize the risk of such damage.

The behaviour of solid wood as it shrinks is, to a large extent, determined by how it is cut from the trunk. If it is cut obliquely across the annual rings (line A-B in Fig 2.14), the board will almost certainly shrink and bend in the direction shown in Fig 2.13. The board is described as being *crown cut*. If the board is cut perpendicularly across the annual rings (line C-D in Fig 2.14), the risk of bending is greatly reduced, as the annual rings are of equal length across the whole length of the board. Such a board is described as *quarter sawn*.

Figure 2.13, a section through the trunk of the tree, shows the annual rings, which are, in effect, circles of wood fibres. When wood shrinks, the annual rings are shrinking in circumference, and the amount of shrinkage in an annual ring increases the further away it is from the centre, because these rings are of greater diameter. Thus, the nearer the

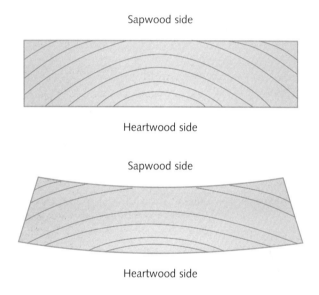

Sapwood side

Heartwood side

Sapwood side

Heartwood side

Fig 2.13 Crown-cut boards will bend away from the heartwood side as they shrink.

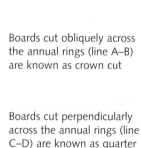

Boards cut obliquely across the annual rings (line A–B) are known as crown cut

Boards cut perpendicularly across the annual rings (line C–D) are known as quarter sawn

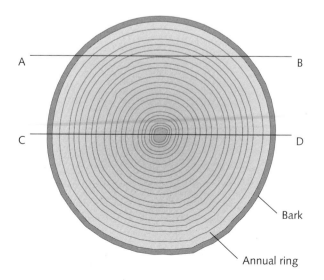

Fig 2.14 Crown-cut and quarter-sawn boards.

Bark

Annual ring

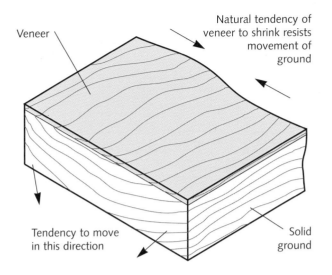

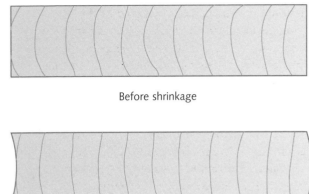

Before shrinkage

After shrinkage

Fig 2.16 Quarter-sawn boards tend not to warp.

Fig 2.15 Veneering the heartwood side of a board will counteract the groundwork's natural tendency to bend in the direction of the sapwood side.

rings are to the heartwood, the less shrinkage they will sustain.

In effect, what is happening in Fig 2.13 is that the wood is bending away from the heartwood. Laying the veneer on the heart side of the board, with its grain running in the same direction as the board's (*see* Fig 2.15), will help to counteract this.

If the board had been quarter sawn this bending would not have happened, though there may have

been some shrinkage in width (*see* Fig 2.16).

To reduce the risk of shrinkage and bending, wide boards should be avoided, and the width made up from two or more boards joined together (*see* Fig 2.17). Notice the way the grain runs in the boards: alternate boards have the heartwood facing in opposite directions, i.e. one board has heartwood facing the top surface, and its neighbour has heartwood facing the bottom surface. The effect of this is to neutralize any rounding. First of all, since each board is relatively narrow, any rounding will be correspondingly less pronounced. Secondly, as

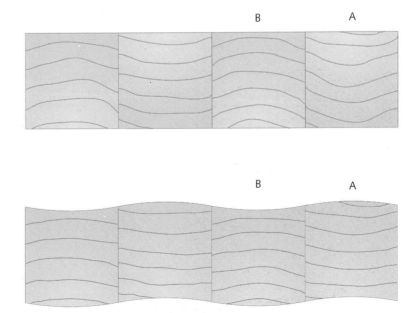

Fig 2.17 Using narrow boards to make up the width of the groundwork reduces the effect of warping. Note that the heartwood and sapwood sides of the boards (labelled A and B respectively) are alternated.

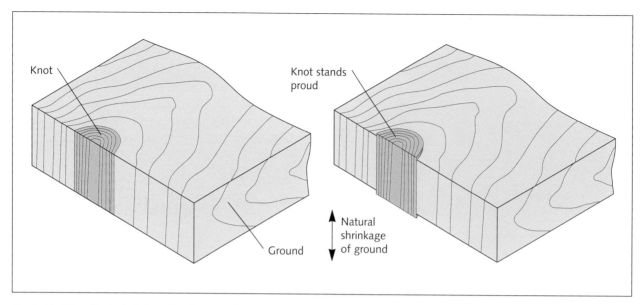

Fig 2.18 The effect of timber shrinkage on knots.

board A will curl upwards, board B will curl downwards and so on across the width of the groundwork (*see* Fig 2.17). The effect is to reduce what would be a major defect to a series of undulations. The narrower the strips of wood making up the width, the less pronounced the undulations will be.

Knots may give rise to problems after laying veneers. As the wood shrinks in thickness, the knot remains intact because its grain direction runs through the thickness of the board. It does not shrink in length and so stands proud of the surface (*see* Fig 2.18). This will eventually show through the veneer. Figure 2.19 shows how to remedy this defect by cutting out a piece of the wood with the knot, gluing in a straight-grained patch, and planing it flush with the surrounding surface. The patch should be the same species of wood as the rest of the ground and the grain should lie in the same direction.

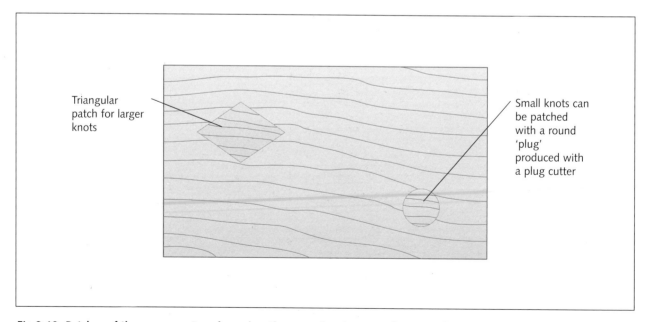

Fig 2.19 Patches of the same species of wood as the groundwork are used to cover knots.

PLYWOOD

Plywood is manufactured by laminating thin layers of wood. This method of construction results in a groundwork that is very stable. There is very little risk of it warping and, provided it is of good quality, the surface provides a good flat base for the veneer.

Figure 2.20 shows how plywood is constructed. The layers in ply always have the grain running at right angles to each other and there is always an odd number of laminations. This means that top and bottom layers will always have the grain running in the same direction. This gives a very strong resistance to warping as each layer is restricting the warping tendencies of its neighbour,

and the forces involved in warping are balanced by the odd number of laminations.

The veneer should always be laid with its grain at right angles to that of the plywood surface in order to maintain the alternating grain direction structure of the ground. This principle does not apply to built up patterns, such as quartering, or to marquetry and parquetry where there is no single grain direction to the veneer.

BLOCKBOARD AND LAMINBOARD

Blockboard is made up of strips of wood about 1in (25mm) wide, glued together with the heartwood facing in alternate directions (*see* Fig 2.21). The top

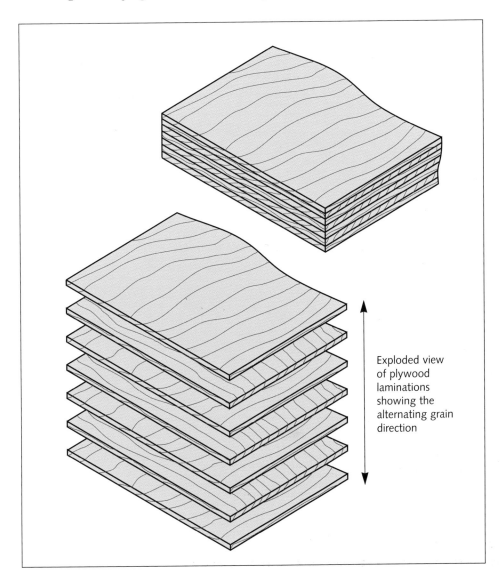

Fig 2.20 Plywood is constructed so that the grain direction of adjacent lamina is at right angles.

Exploded view of plywood laminations showing the alternating grain direction

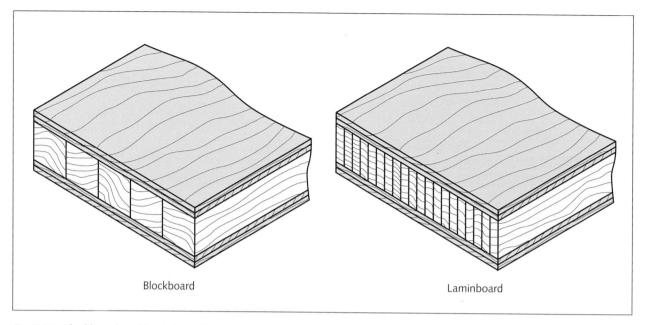

Blockboard

Laminboard

Fig 2.21 Blockboard and laminboard have a similar construction, but the core of laminboard is made up of much narrower strips. As a result, laminboard is a much better material, but also more expensive.

and bottom surfaces are then laminated to provide a large, flat surface, the grain direction of which runs the same way as that of the core. Laminboard (*see* Fig 2.21) is similar except that the core is made up of much thinner pieces of wood, about ¼in (6mm) wide. When veneering such boards, the veneer's grain should run at right angles to the surface layer.

CHIPBOARD AND MEDIUM DENSITY FIBREBOARD (MDF)

Both these manufactured boards are produced from wood fibres bonded together under very high pressure. The result is a dense core with a smooth outer surface. Medium density fibreboard (MDF), the top board in Fig 2.22, is made up of very fine

Fig 2.22 Top: medium density fibreboard (MDF). Bottom: chipboard.

wood fibres. In fact, the fibres used to make MDF have the texture of cotton wool. Chipboard, the bottom board in Fig 2.22, is made up of coarser fibres. The outer surfaces of these boards are smooth, although that of chipboard is usually less so, and so present excellent surfaces for veneering. Their main advantage is that they have no natural tendency to warp, therefore there is no restriction on veneer grain direction.

ADHESIVES

The traditional adhesive for veneers was pearl glue (also known as Scotch glue and animal glue), but there is now a whole range of alternatives that in many cases are better. However, pearl glue is still a very valuable part of the restorer's kit and is the only glue that can be used with the veneer hammer (*see* Chapters 3 and 5). The glues suitable for use in veneering are described below.

PEARL GLUE

Pearl glue is the most common modern name for what some readers may remember as good old fashioned Scotch glue, but it is much easier to prepare (*see* page 20). The glue derives its name from the way it is sold – as small pellets called pearls.

When prepared properly, the glue will take the form of a very stiff gel when cold, but will liquefy when heated. The advantage of this is that you may apply glue to the groundwork and leave it to cool and gel, giving you time to place the veneer accurately without it sticking. The glue can then be reheated and the veneer pressed down. This is the principle of both hammer and heated caul veneering (*see* Chapters 3 and 5). Most other adhesives, while offering some time advantage, do not leave much time for error. If you make a mistake with pearl glue, you can simply heat the veneer with an iron and lift it off as the glue melts. This can be somewhat messy, but it does allow you to correct your mistakes more easily than with any other type of glue.

There are very good reasons why pearl glue should remain an important part of the veneerer's kit. These are listed in the table, right, along with some of the disadvantages.

ADVANTAGES AND DISADVANTAGES OF PEARL GLUE

ADVANTAGES	DISADVANTAGES
● Relatively cheap when compared with other adhesives suitable for veneering.	● Putrefies if kept in its gel form for longer than a few days (especially in summer).
● Indefinite shelf life when kept in its dry form (i.e. as pearls).	● Tends to swell and expand if too much heat and water are used when the veneer is laid. As the work dries, shrinkage will occur and this may cause veneer joints to open.
● Necessary for sympathetic restoration work, and very useful for repairing small areas of damaged veneer.	
● Presses and other complicated equipment are not necessary for many veneering tasks.	● Heated press or caul (*see* Chapters 3 and 5) are needed for marquetry and parquetry.
● Allows a long working time because the glue can be liquefied by heating while work is in progress.	● Water solubility and heat sensitivity make items using this glue vulnerable (e.g. table tops).
● Water-soluble, therefore easy to clean up surplus glue.	● Being dark in colour, veneer joints may be more noticeable, especially with light coloured veneers.

PREPARATION

Figures 2.23 to 2.25 illustrate how pearl glue is prepared for use. It is necessary to soak the pellets in water for a couple of hours, during which time they absorb the water and swell to at least twice the size of the dry pellets. It is difficult to judge the amount of glue you will need for any one job, so the following is only a rough guide.

PREPARING PEARL GLUE

1 Half fill a jam jar with glue pellets, then fill to the brim with water (this proportion should be followed with any quantity of glue you make up) and leave to stand for at least two hours. After this time, all or nearly all of the water will have been absorbed and the swollen pellets will fill the container.

2 Transfer the swollen pellets of glue into a traditional woodworker's glue pot (*see* Fig 2.24). If you do not have a glue pot you can make up some other form of double boiler arrangement, such as a

Fig 2.24 After absorbing water, the pearls at least double their volume. Even though the swollen pearls are sitting proud of the glue pot, the liquid glue occupies less space.

tin can in a pan of water. The important thing is that when the glue is heated, it is not done over a direct heat, which would burn it. Heating up the glue using a double boiler or the glue pot ensures that the glue only gets as hot as boiling water. The other advantage is that the hot water will maintain the glue in a hot liquefied state for a long time during use, because it is often necessary to take the glue away from the source of heat to use it. If you use an improvised arrangement, keep the glue in the hot water to maintain its hot liquid state.

3 Pearl glue is always applied to the groundwork with a brush, and special glue brushes can be bought for this purpose. The hot glue should run off the brush in a steady stream, as shown in Fig 2.25. If the glue is too thick and falls as individual blobs, water can be added; if it is too thin; and breaks up before it hits the pot, continue heating it to evaporate the surplus water. Because the glue thickens as water evaporates, you will need to add a little extra water from time to time to maintain

Fig 2.23 Pearl glue is so called because of its appearance before it is prepared for use.

Fig 2.25 The perfect consistency for glue: it runs off the glue brush in a steady stream.

fluidity. You may not use all the glue in any one job, but you can re-use what is left over by reheating it when needed, keeping in mind that the glue is perishable.

POLYVINYL ACETATE (PVA)

Polyvinyl acetate (PVA) is a water-based adhesive that has many uses. It has a fairly short working time (perhaps about 10 minutes), decreasing if the air temperature is warm. Typical well-known brand names include Evo-Stik Resin W and Unibond. Since the setting time is fairly short, you will need to work quickly to lay veneers with some form of press (*see* Chapter 3).

PVA glue has high convenience value in that it is readily available from any DIY store in small quantities and in bulk – up to 1gal (5l). Complex veneering tasks involving joining two or more veneers together will need to be done prior to laying. Originally, all PVA glues were water-soluble

even after drying. Now, there are water-resistant PVA glues that will not be redissolved by water after drying.

PVA is a good general purpose adhesive and can be used for any veneering work, though it does require a means of clamping until the glue has dried – usually some form of press (*see* Chapters 3 and 5).

ADVANTAGES AND DISADVANTAGES OF PVA

ADVANTAGES	DISADVANTAGES
● Very easy to obtain from local sources such as DIY stores.	● Short working time means that there is little room for error.
● Long shelf life if kept in airtight container.	
● Water-soluble, therefore easy to clean off surplus (this excludes the water resistant types).	
● Lack of heat and moisture means that veneers are less likely to swell and then shrink.	

CONTACT ADHESIVES

As their name implies, these glues bond instantly with the veneer as soon as it comes into contact with the glued groundwork. There is no room for error! You will not be able to remove the veneer in one piece once it has been placed on the groundwork. This makes contact adhesives ideal for jobs where it might be difficult to maintain sufficient pressure – small-scale shaped work, for example. Reliable bonding occurs if both the veneer and groundwork are glued (*see* Chapter 5). Contact adhesives are based on very powerful, volatile solvents and are not particularly pleasant materials to use routinely for veneered work. They certainly should not be used without plenty of ventilation.

ADVANTAGES AND DISADVANTAGES OF CONTACT ADHESIVES

ADVANTAGES	DISADVANTAGES
● Do not require pressing equipment.	● Very powerful solvents make them unpleasant to work with for an extended period.
● Not water based, therefore veneers will not swell or shrink.	● Expensive when compared with many other forms of adhesive.
● Instantaneous bonding is ideal for awkward shapes that would be difficult to keep under pressure.	● No room for error – veneer must be placed accurately first time.
● Resistant to heat, so good for such things as table tops.	● Not suitable for use with built up veneers, e.g. parquetry and marquetry. Only suitable for laying single pieces of veneer (the pressure used to make good contact may open any veneer joints.

CASCAMITE

Cascamite is bought as a powder that you mix with water to form a paste. It is based on a chemical called urea-formaldehyde, and its adhesive action is brought about by a catalyst that hardens the paste by chemical reaction. This sets the glue after a few hours, but it still requires time to cure.

Once mixed with water, it has a usable life of a few hours, so there is an extended working time. It is also waterproof when set and so is ideal for use where there are fairly humid conditions. As an example, classic car enthusiasts who wish to restore veneered trims should use this glue.

Apart from such specialized uses, Cascamite is not the ideal material for veneering. Since it hardens by chemical action rather than through the evaporation of a solvent, it cannot be softened once it has hardened. This presents problems when

newly veneered work needs to be cleaned off. If any glue finds its way onto the surface during the process of laying the veneer, it is very difficult to remove as it is as hard as glass. Contaminated areas will also be difficult to stain a different colour.

ADVANTAGES AND DISADVANTAGES OF CASCAMITE

ADVANTAGES	DISADVANTAGES
● Slow setting time, therefore working time quite long, but heavily dependent on room temperature – sets quicker in warmer environments.	● Expensive.
● Ideal for work that will be subjected to higher levels of atmospheric humidity, e.g. car dashboards. Also very resistant to hot objects such as food dishes.	● May present particularly difficult surface finishing problems should a veneered surface become contaminated during laying.
● Long shelf life, provided it is stored as a powder in an airtight container.	

GLUE FILM

This is an innovative product in which the glue is in the form of a thin film on backing paper. It is sold in rolls and may be bought by the metre or in bulk. For some straightforward work it is a useful material. The emphasis is on the word *straightforward*. While it is good for laying single sheets of veneer, anything more complicated, such as laying two or more veneers joined together, can be difficult.

The usual method for using this glue is to iron it onto the groundwork, running a moderately hot clothes iron over the backing paper. After cooling, the backing paper is carefully peeled away to leave a film of glue bonded to the groundwork. In fact, it takes some practice to be able to do this effectively over a large surface, without leaving areas of glue on the paper rather than on the work. There is an alternative method that I find easier.

USING GLUE FILM – ALTERNATIVE METHOD

1 Peel the film of glue away from the backing sheet. (The glue layer is quite thick, so can be removed without much difficulty.)

2 Place the film over the groundwork, then place the veneer over that.

3 Iron the veneer onto the ground with a clothes iron. (As the glue is heated only once, there is a guaranteed thickness of glue.)

(*See* Chapter 5 for a more detailed discussion on using glue film.)

ADVANTAGES AND DISADVANTAGES OF GLUE FILM

ADVANTAGES	DISADVANTAGES
● Easy to use, after some practice.	● Expensive.
● A clean adhesive – no requirement to clean off surplus glue from veneered surfaces.	● Not suitable for use on work requiring veneers to be joined.
● Waterproof.	
● Indefinite shelf life.	

ABRASIVES

As veneers are generally so thin, the finer grades of abrasives are used in surface finishing (*see* Chapter 11). While there are a number of different abrasive papers available, one consistent feature is the system of sizing the particles: this grit size is given on the back of the abrasive. The best sizes for

veneered work are 180, 240 and 320. Choice of paper is a matter of personal preference, but it is worth looking at the alternatives.

GLASS PAPER

This is one of the cheapest abrasive papers. Particles of glass, the abrasive, are bonded to the paper. The problem with it is that the glass wears down very quickly, so it rapidly loses its cut.

GARNET PAPER

Particles of garnet stone are used as the abrasive here, giving this paper excellent cutting power. It is also very long lasting, so represents very good value for money.

ALUMINIUM OXIDE (PRODUCTION PAPER)

Aluminium oxide, a man-made material, is very hard indeed; hard enough to be used on metal and thus ideal for use on the harder woods.

SILICON CARBIDE (LUBRISIL)

Silicon carbide is an extremely hard mineral that is a commonly used abrasive by metal and wood workers. Waterproof silicon carbide papers are better known as 'wet-or-dry', and while these can be used with wood as well as metal, many wood workers prefer to use the version specifically designed for use with wood. All papers, especially the finer grits, become clogged with wood dust as they do their work. This means that they must be cleared of dust regularly. Lubrisil paper, the wood workers' silicon carbide paper, contains its own lubricant which helps to keep it clear of dust and enables it to be cleared more easily. This is an expensive paper, but has exceptional cutting power and durability.

NYLON MESH ABRASIVE

Nylon mesh abrasives, available in several grades, are ideal for cutting back a polish coat without leaving obvious scratches that will show through the next coat. These abrasives are popular in the auto refinishing trade where their flexibility makes them ideal for smoothing shaped areas. They are also good for smoothing veneer prior to polishing. Because of their open texture they do not clog with dust, but their greatest advantage is their longevity – they simply go on and on. Excellent value for money.

POLISHES

The general principles of polishing solid wood and polishing veneer are much the same. The main difference concerns work in which there are different veneers used, particularly if there are contrasting colours that need to be preserved. (*See* Chapter 11.)

The most common polishing materials are described below.

WAX POLISH

This polish is extremely easy to apply, but suffers from a general lack of durability. Nevertheless, it will produce a soft lustre that is ideal for, say, marquetry pictures that won't be handled a great deal. Such pictures would suffer from the effect of a high lustre finish that might create distracting reflections.

OIL POLISH

Like wax polish, oiling results in a pleasant low-lustre finish, but has the advantage of being rather more durable. Danish or Tung oil are ideal because they are light (both in colour and consistency) and readily absorbed into the wood. They also dry quite quickly.

FRENCH POLISH

French polish is based on a solution of shellac in alcohol. It provides a fast-drying finish that forms a hard film over the work, giving a better protective finish than wax. Most people think of french polish as the so-called 'piano' finish – a high mirror gloss. In fact, it is much more versatile than this and can be applied in such a way as to create a range of finishes, from very dull to very high gloss. The finish required depends very much on the nature of the work. Marquetry pictures, as already discussed, tend to look better if the polish has a low lustre. There are no hard and fast rules though, with much depending on personal preference. The one exception to this is restoration work. Here, the restored areas must match the original areas as closely as possible.

Colour is an important consideration. French polish is available in a range of colours, from dark (garnet polish) to pale amber (transparent, sometimes called pale transparent). The latter is ideal for work where colour change is to be kept to a minimum, for example, marquetry where woods of contrasting colours will be used.

French polish is not resistant to heat, water or solvents and lengthy exposure to any of these will result in damage – hot plates and cups will mark the polished surface very badly. If a french polished piece is kept in damp conditions (e.g. a cold, damp garage) for any length of time, it may cloud over as the dampness affects the polish. However, the classic example of water damage is the over-watered pot plant. Surplus water may run onto the polished surface and be left there. The inevitable outcome of this is white ring marks and spots. In very bad cases, the marks will be dark where the water has penetrated the polish and stained the wood beneath. In the worst case scenario, if water-soluble glue has been used, the veneer will also lift.

POLYURETHANE VARNISH

This hard-wearing, easy-to-apply finish takes some beating, although it does suffer from a mixed reputation. While french polish carries a certain mystique and a reputation for high quality, polyurethane has been regarded as representing the opposite end of the spectrum. Nothing could be further from the truth. In fact, polyurethane has many advantages over french polish: it is tougher, resists mechanical damage better and is resistant to heat and water, making it ideal for table tops.

CATALYSED LACQUERS

There are a number of polishes on the market that work by chemical action. By adding a catalyst (a chemical that speeds up the chemical reaction of another), the resulting polish becomes so hard that very little will damage it. Such lacquers can be applied by brush or spray.

As with other polishes, the lacquer dries as the solvent evaporates, but over the following hours, the extra hardness of a catalysed lacquer develops.

The chemical reaction renders the film of polish impervious to most commonly available solvents, and to relatively high temperatures. Because of these qualities, catalysed lacquers are ideal for items, such as coffee tables, that will have to endure heavy use.

PROPERTIES OF FINISHING MATERIALS

	WAX POLISH	OIL POLISH	FRENCH POLISH	POLYURETHANE	CATALYSED LACQUERS
EASE OF APPLICATION	Very easy and quick.	Very easy, but time-consuming as many coats are needed.	Requires considerable skill to apply, but this can be achieved with practice.	Not difficult to apply, but some care needed if the end result is to be pleasing.	Can be brushed or sprayed on, but the solvent is very volatile and a good finish can be difficult to achieve.
RESISTANCE TO HEAT	None.	Resists heat, but may be marked. Any marks can be eliminated by applying another coat of oil polish.	Does not have high resistance and is easily marked by hot dishes.	Resistant to hot objects, but anything straight from the oven may mark the surface.	Very resistant.
RESISTANCE TO WATER	None.	Resists water, provided many coats of oil have been applied and allowed to harden.	Not resistant to water left standing on its surface.	Resistant provided several coats have been applied.	Very resistant.
RESISTANCE TO MECHANICAL DAMAGE	None, but a new coat of wax may remedy any marks.	None, but a new coat of oil may remedy any marks.	Fairly resistant, but it does scratch quite easily.	Resistant.	Very resistant, but can be brittle.
EASE OF REPAIR	Very easy. Simply apply more wax polish.	Very easy. Simply apply more oil polish.	Damaged areas can often be repaired without stripping the whole surface.	Damaged areas can often be repaired without stripping the whole surface.	Lacquers are resistant to paint and varnish strippers which can present serious problems in repairing a surface.

3

TOOLS AND EQUIPMENT

♦ CUTTING TOOLS

♦ VENEER LAYING TOOLS

CUTTING TOOLS

KNIVES

The main qualities required in a veneer cutting knife are:

- extreme sharpness of the cutting edge;
- extreme thinness across the cutting blade;
- a very sharp point to enable the knife to get into tight areas (such as the points of diamonds in parquetry) and to make tight turns; and
- comfortable to hold for ease of use.

VENEER KNIVES

Both knives shown in Fig 3.1 use the same replaceable blade, differing only in their handle shapes. Which shape is better is a matter of preference, although the thicker handle is more comfortable for heavy cutting or prolonged use. Note the shape of the blades in Fig 3.1. These surgical blades are available from any craft shop. The blade shown is ideal for cutting veneers. It is extremely thin, and the long cutting edge makes an acute angle with the straight back of the blade. A fine cut with a shallow angle is essential for good joining of veneers, as the finer and

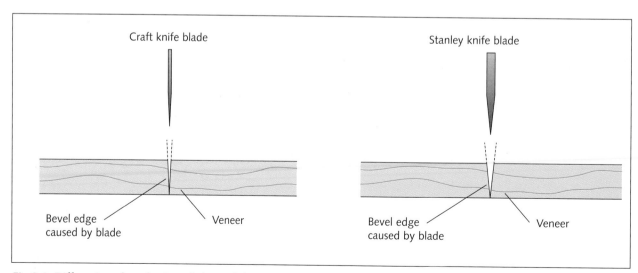

Fig 3.1 Different angles of cut made by craft knives and heavier blades.

shallower the cut, the closer the joints will be. The blades of heavier duty knives, such as Stanley knives, are too thick and have a cutting angle that is too deep for veneering purposes. The dotted lines in Fig 3.1 indicate the angle of the cut made by the blades.

When cutting the veneer, always ensure that the knife is held perpendicular to it. Effective cutting is achieved by inserting the point of the blade only, and pulling it through the length of the cut. This ensures that the width of the cut is very narrow,

and allows fairly sharp curves to be made, as is required in marquetry. The blade will compress the veneer on each side, but the fibres will tend to relax and swell again with the glue, closing up the joint. If the knife is held off the vertical, there is the risk, especially in complex, built-up patterns, that the joints will be poorly fitting. Figure 3.2 shows the sort of difficulties that may arise.

Even though they are described as replaceable, these blades can be repeatedly sharpened. Use an oilstone to hone the back of the blade as shown in

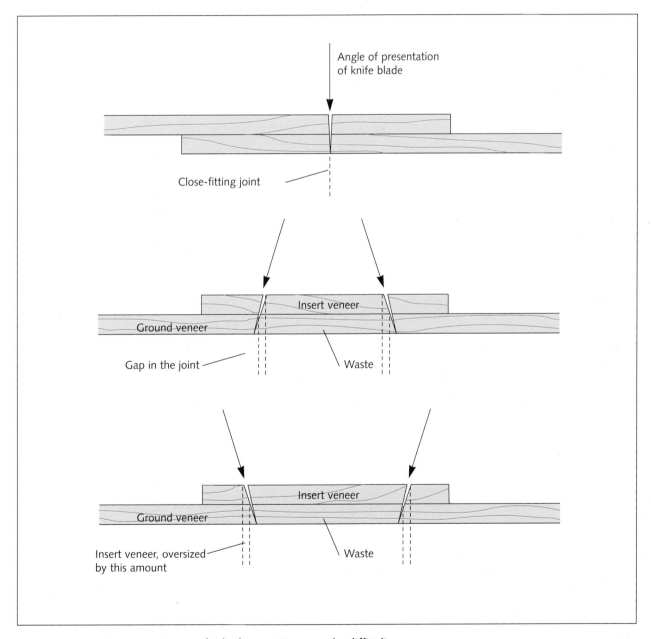

Fig 3.2 Cutting pieces to exact size for built-up patterns can be difficult.

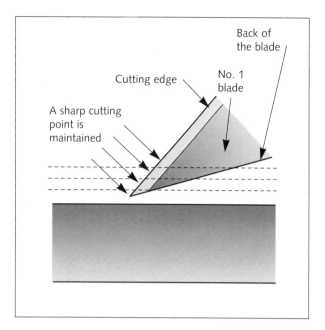

Fig 3.3 Sharpen the blade regularly on an oilstone to keep it in top condition.

Fig 3.3. As the back is worn down (as indicated by the dotted lines), a sharp point is always maintained.

THE CUTTING SURFACE

The surface on which the veneer is cut has a significant effect on the life of the blade. While a hard surface will rapidly dull the edge, one that is too soft will not give a clean cut in the veneer, and will itself eventually disintegrate. Special cutting mats that provide a firm surface to support the veneer, but allow the knife to penetrate it, thus conserving the edge of the blade, can be bought. When the blade is removed from the surface of the mat the cut closes up and its surface is restored. However, such mats are expensive, and I generally use scrap veneer or card.

STRAIGHTEDGES

Most of the decorative techniques of veneering rely upon close-fitting joints between adjacent pieces. Often these joints are straight, in which case accuracy in their cutting is vital. A good, reliable straightedge is needed. The engineers' rule and the straightedge (*see* Fig 3.4) are ideal and can be bought in several lengths to suit the work undertaken. The straightedge shown is especially useful for several reasons. One edge is calibrated in millimetres for measuring, while the other has a hard, stainless steel insert that is an accurate straightedge for cutting. The main material is aluminium, so it is lightweight. Furthermore, there is a non-slip silicone insert on the under surface – a very useful feature on a straightedge, which it is vital to keep still.

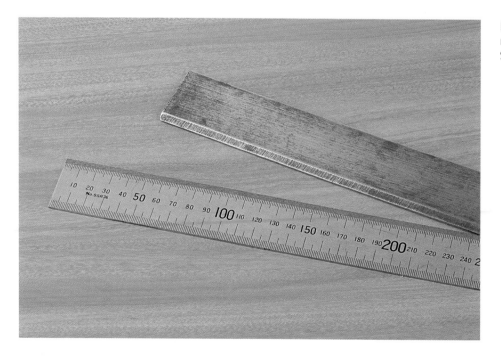

Fig 3.4 Top: Engineers' rule. Bottom: Straightedge.

Fig 3.5 The curved blade of the veneer saw.

A straightedge will need to remain true and be able to stand up to considerable wear. This means that it ought to be made of metal. The standard wooden or plastic rule will not do because its edge will be eroded by the action of the veneer knife. As far as length is concerned, this will depend on the nature of the work, but two sizes are likely to be very useful: 18in (45cm) and 3ft (100cm).

VENEER SAWS

Obviously, this is not a knife, but it performs the same function in situations where a veneer knife would be unsuitable. (*See* Using the Veneer Knife, Chapter 4.) Veneer saws are ideal for use in place of a knife with the thicker sawn veneers and for thinner veneers that are brittle or particularly hard. The thin blade of the saw does not have any 'set' so it does not cut a wide kerf. Notice, from Fig 3.5, that the blade is curved: this prevents it snagging as it is drawn across the veneer. The curve ensures a smooth cutting action and the fine teeth ensure a clean cut, so that even on the most brittle of veneers, a gentle sawing action will result in a clean cut, without splintering.

FRETSAWS

Knives are fine for the straight cuts associated with parquetry or when laying with straight joints (e.g. book-matching or quartering), but for complicated

work, a fretsaw is really the only tool that will create the shapes easily. These saws have very fine cutting blades so that the veneers form close joints when laid. The blades can be so fine as to resemble wire and will break very easily in inexperienced hands. Both wood cutting and metal cutting blades are available.

Hand fretsaws are relatively cheap. The saw must be held vertically in one hand while the veneer 'pack' is manipulated with the other. This is not an easy task, and it is worth spending a lot of time practising with waste veneers, but with some experience, you will master the knack. The action is to move the saw up and down with small strokes. The veneer should be moved into the blade, *not* the other way round, but without pressure, as this will break the delicate blade. (*See* Figs 3.6–3.8.)

The fretsaw shown in Fig 3.6 has a deep throat (i.e. the distance between the blade and the side of the frame directly opposite). A balance must be struck between the depth of the throat, which allows larger pieces of marquetry panel to be worked, and the overall weight and balance of the tool.

This, of course, is not an issue with a machine fretsaw. Note that the hand saw is used with a home-made cutting table (*see* Fig 3.6). The 'V' shape cut from the table enables the veneer pack to be well supported while the saw is able to cut deep within the pack of veneers.

Fig 3.6 Technique for hand cutting with a fretsaw.

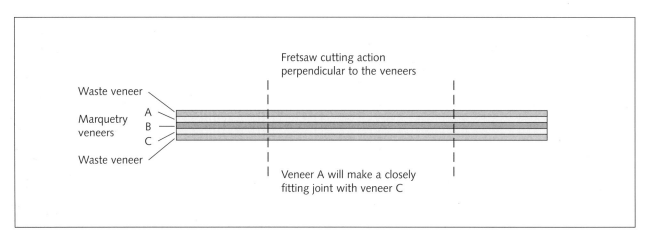

Fretsaw cutting action
perpendicular to the veneers

Waste veneer

Marquetry
veneers

A
B
C

Waste veneer

Veneer A will make a closely
fitting joint with veneer C

Fig 3.7 Keeping the fretsaw vertical ensures that veneer C makes a close joint with veneer A.

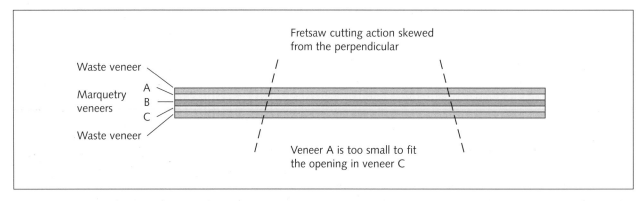

Fretsaw cutting action skewed
from the perpendicular

Waste veneer

Marquetry
veneers

A
B
C

Waste veneer

Veneer A is too small to fit
the opening in veneer C

Fig 3.8 When the fretsaw is used off the vertical, veneer A may be significantly smaller than the space for it in veneer C,
leading to an ill-fitting joint.

Machine reciprocating fretsaws have the advantage of enabling the operator to hold the veneers with both hands. However, this has to be set against the reduced level of control over the cutting action itself. This may be a particular problem with very intricate designs. All the same, if you are producing large numbers of marquetry panels, the machine will make the work much faster. Practise with the machine before attempting important work.

MARQUETRY 'DONKEYS'

The marquetry 'donkey' (*see* Fig 1.4) is an alternative to the hand-held fretsaw. They are operated by a foot treadle, keeping both hands free to manipulate the veneer. Their other advantage is the accuracy with which they can cut the veneer. The 'donkey', once properly set up, is very accurate and keeps the blade perpendicular to the surface. These machines are now rare, but it is possible to make your own and plans for making one can be obtained from specialist suppliers (*see* Suppliers on page 156).

The blade in some donkeys is mounted to cut horizontally rather than vertically. The horizontal model allows the operator to be seated more comfortably.

The purpose of a fretsaw is to enable all the veneers used in a marquetry piece to be cut at the same time, like a sandwich, so that the pieces are then unpacked and reassembled in their positions afterwards. (*See* Chapter 10.) The donkey's accuracy allows repeat patterns to be cut all at the same time.

CUTTING GAUGE

The cutting gauge is frequently used during hammer veneering for trimming centre panels ready to take a cross-banding or similar edging veneer. It resembles a marking gauge, but has a small blade rather than a pin, so that it works by cutting at a fixed distance from the stock (*see* Fig 3.9). This enables a constant distance to be achieved when trimming veneer panels.

PLANE AND SHOOTING BOARDS

Where veneer joints will be laid by press rather than by veneer hammer, there is a role for planes. In partnership with a 'shooting board' (*see* Fig 3.10), the

Fig 3.9 The cutting gauge enables consistent cutting at a fixed distance.

Fig 3.10 A long plane (a No. 6 or 7) used with a shooting board will ensure true edges for jointing.

edges of the veneers used in book-matching and quartering can be made true using a plane, to give a very close joint. In the case of the thicker, sawn veneers, this is the only satisfactory way of preparing straight edges for jointing. Particular care needs to be exercised in preparing quartered veneers, as each of the joining edges must be square with its adjacent edge if they are to make a good joint – this is where the shooting board comes into its own. The general principles of constructing a shooting board are shown in Fig 3.11. Fence A must be at right angles to edge B of the top board C. Ideally, it should be recessed into C, but since veneering work places very little strain on A, it can be securely screwed (I never use glue because, in the event of damage, it is relatively easy to replace components). The exploded view in Fig 3.11 shows that the edge of C is undercut slightly. Sawdust will collect in this space rather than on the board, D, where it might interfere with the action of the plane.

ROUTER

The router is a most versatile tool. As far as veneering is concerned, the tool is invaluable for trimming the excess veneer around the edge of the work and also for trenching out grooves to take inlays. This is quite apart from its more usual work of shaping edges after they have been applied to the veneered groundwork (*see* Chapter 5).

The power router has become an increasingly important part of the veneerers' tool kit. The availability of a wide range of straight-cutting bits allows rapid cutting of grooves to take inlays while other specialized bits allow excess veneer to be trimmed from the edges of the work. Consequently, for both areas of work there is a considerable saving in time. The bit shown in Fig 3.12 is a $\frac{1}{4}$in (6mm) straight tungsten cutter which can be used for producing the groove for an inlay or, with the use of the router's fence, to trim excess veneer on square or rectangular work. For work that is

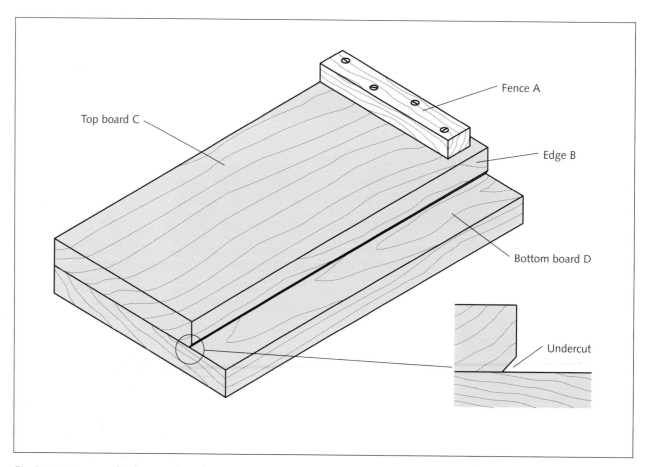

Fig 3.11 Home-made shooting board.

curved, such as circular or oval table tops, a specially designed laminate trimmer is required (*see* Chapter 5).

SCRATCHSTOCK

This, the traditional means of producing a groove for an inlay, is still useful on occasions. The process is laborious, but there are situations, such as working on very narrow surfaces, where a router is not up to the job, or where the inlay is of a size for which there is not an appropriate cutter.

A scratchstock can be easily made. The tool in Fig 3.13 consists of two pieces of L-shaped wood screwed together, holding a home-made cutter. The cutters can be made from old saw blades, cut and filed to shape.

The scratchstock is operated by holding the fence against the edge of the work and moving it

Fig 3.12 Specialized bits adapt the power router for particular jobs.

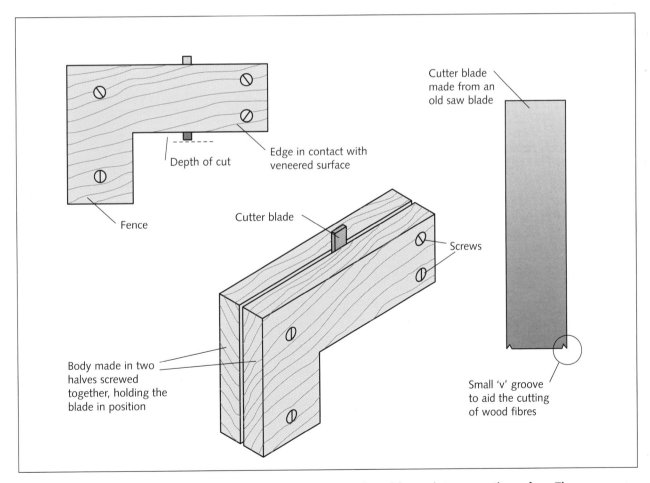

Cutter blade made from an old saw blade

Depth of cut

Edge in contact with veneered surface

Fence

Cutter blade

Screws

Body made in two halves screwed together, holding the blade in position

Small 'v' groove to aid the cutting of wood fibres

Fig 3.13 The scratchstock produces grooves by moving it backwards and forwards to scrape the surface. The adjustable blade determines the depth.

backwards and forwards to scrape the groove out of the surface (hence the name of the tool). The depth of cut is determined by how far the blade protrudes below the horizontal member of the tool (*see* inset in Fig 3.13).

The main problem with this tool is its tendency to create a ragged edge because of the scraping action. This can be alleviated by filing a 'V' shape in the cutting edge, as shown in Fig 3.13. The two sides of the cutting edge will cut the wood fibres rather than simply scrape them and it should lead to a cleaner groove.

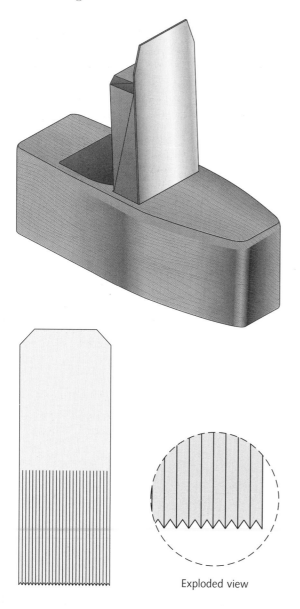

Exploded view

Fig 3.14 A toothing plane. Grooves in the plane iron create a serrated edge.

PARQUETRY JIGS

Parquetry relies very heavily on the accurate cutting and laying of geometric shapes. In most cases, squares and diamonds are the basic shapes from which other patterns are built up. Since these shapes will need to tessellate without any gaps, every piece of the built-up pattern must be spot-on, with absolute accuracy in the cutting of angles. This is especially important when the pattern is covering a large area, as any small discrepancy will tend to become exaggerated as the errors become multiplied. The use of jigs will enable you to cut component pieces with consistent angles and sizes. Assuming the jig is itself constructed accurately, it will minimize inaccuracies. (*See* Fig 9.9, page 108.)

The spacers must be identical in width in order for the straightedge to produce uniform strips. Also, the wooden stop against which the veneer butts *must* have its edge planed straight and true. This stop is simply screwed onto the base board so that it can be removed to replace it, or to plane the edge true, should any damage occur.

VENEER-LAYING TOOLS

TOOTHING PLANE

In the days before plywood and particle boards, when veneers were laid onto a solid ground, any irregularity in the surface would have caused some difficulties when bonding. When veneers were routinely cut by saw, the roughness caused by the saw was also problematic for bonding. The toothing plane was, therefore, an essential tool for preparing both the ground and the veneer surface. It removed these irregularities and provided a keyed surface for improved bonding. This is less of a problem with modern materials and knife-cut veneers, but for restoration or authentic copy work, it remains essential. Also, if you are working with thick, saw-cut veneers, the plane will remove the marks left by the saw blade.

A toothing plane is quite small. It is held with one hand for working over the surface of a solid ground. This is done in a random fashion, but ensuring that the whole surface is covered. The blade is vertical and protrudes from the sole of the plane by only a very small amount.

The action is one of scouring the wood surface. The cutting edge is serrated so that it creates many small grooves that both even out irregularities and leave the key for gluing (*see* Fig 3.14).

VENEER HAMMER

This is quite the wrong name for the tool as it is in no way used with such an action. It owes more to a 'squeegee' than to a hammer. The hammer head has a bull-nosed strip of brass set into its edge. It is this which is used to press the veneer down onto the ground, to squeeze out surplus glue and ensure good contact between the surfaces (*see* Fig 3.15). As a traditional veneering tool it was designed for use with animal glue, but it can be used with contact adhesives. Other glues are not suitable candidates because they do not 'grab' the veneer on contact. Once the hammer passes over an area the pressure is released and contact may be lost between veneer and ground. For non-contact adhesives, a veneer press will be needed.

Fig 3.15 The brass strip in the veneer hammer creates the pressure to bind the glue and veneer.

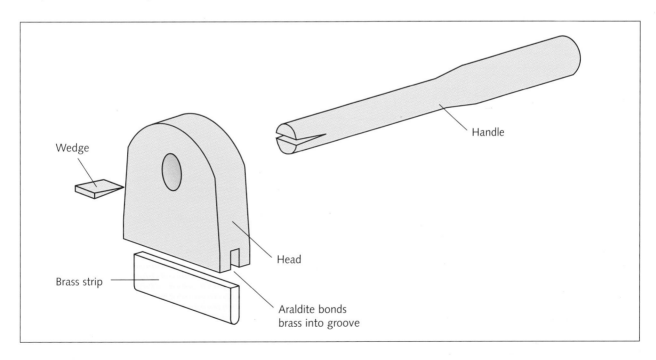

Fig 3.16 A home-made veneer hammer.

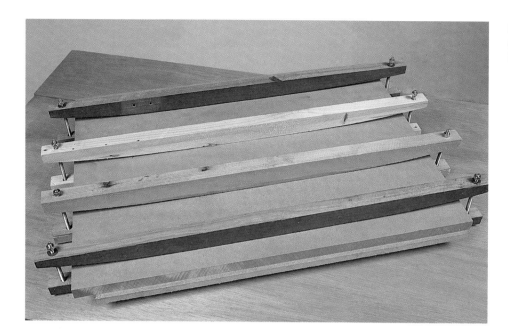

Fig 3.17 The caul press –
a low-cost method, using
bolts rather than clamps.

The hammer can be held in a variety of ways, depending on the preference of the worker. The grip shown in Fig 3.15 is my preferred method, as it allows considerable pressure to be exerted.

Veneer hammers are available commercially, or can be home-made. The advantage of making your own is that you can have a number of them in two or three different sizes to cope with different work and to fit your own grip. If you do choose to make your own, you must use brass or other non-ferrous metal, as steel will rust and may stain certain veneers.

CAUL PRESS

The caul method is a low-cost alternative to a large press, and is very much a cottage approach to veneer pressing. The work is placed between two boards (the cauls), which are larger than the work itself. Pressure is exerted by a set of paired bearers, or battens, laid across the top board and beneath the bottom board. The shape of the bearers is significant. The load-exerting edge should be bowed slightly. (In Fig 3.18, such a curvature is greatly exaggerated for clarity.) The

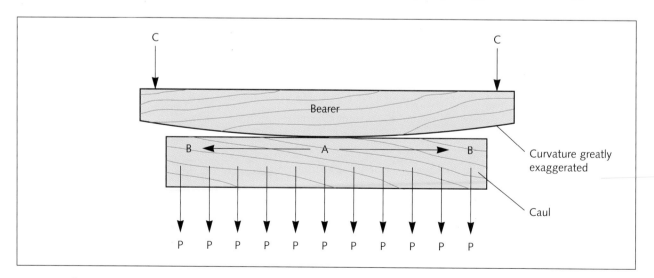

Fig 3.18 The curve of the bearers ensures that excess glue is squeezed out, minimizing the risk of trapped glue causing lumps and creases in the veneer.

purpose of this curvature is to ensure that the bearer applies downward pressure, P, progressively, from the centre to the edge (i.e. in the directions A-B), as the clamp pressure, C, is exerted. The clamps are tightened slowly to allow time for any surplus glue to be squeezed outwards. This ensures that surplus glue is squeezed out rather than trapped, with the risk of creating a lump or a crease in the veneer. It has to be said though, that it is bad practice to use so much glue that such an occurrence might take place!

The more pairs of cauls you have the better, but for most people, this is determined by the number of clamps they own – or have begged – as each pair of bearers requires a set of clamps.

VENEER PRESS

For most small workshops where only occasional work is carried out, the caul method is perfectly adequate, but for production work in commercial workshops, larger industrial quality presses will be needed. Some of these machines are heated, so the resin glues used by commercial ventures set rather more quickly than would be the case with a 'cold' press.

HAND-SCREW PRESS

This is a very simple device whereby pressure on the work is maintained by the action of a heavy metal plate which is pressed down onto the work. Pressure is exerted using a heavily threaded column which is operated by turning the long handle at the top. This equipment is ideal for small work, and quite large presses can be constructed by using more than one hand screw to ensure that an even pressure is exerted over the whole veneered surface.

In commercial workshops, for production runs where the rate of output is important, the pressure plates are heated to speed up the setting of the adhesive. Commercial presses take up a great deal of space, and for amateurs and people carrying out one-off veneering projects, a machine of this kind would be a heavy investment.

While you can make your own veneer press (the separate components are readily available), the results are not always satisfactory, as it is difficult to prevent the arrangement distorting as pressure is applied.

VACUUM BAG PRESS

Shaped work can be problematic. During pressing, the veneer must be kept in contact with the ground for the entire drying period of the glue. Flat surfaces are relatively easy to deal with, but maintaining contact between a shaped ground and the veneer is a different proposition altogether – compound shapes, particularly.

A vacuum bag press does away with the need for a large number of clamps for larger surfaces. It is also able to deliver a great deal of pressure over the whole surface more evenly than the caul method. However, unlike the sand box, it is suitable only for cold setting glues.

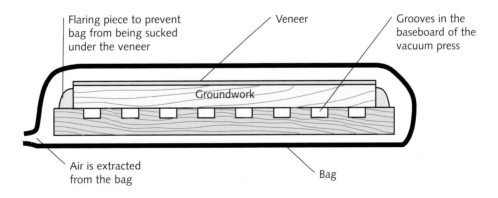

Flaring piece to prevent bag from being sucked under the veneer

Veneer

Grooves in the baseboard of the vacuum press

Groundwork

Air is extracted from the bag

Bag

Fig 3.19 The baseboard of a vacuum press has grooves running across its surface to assist air extraction.

A vacuum bag press, including the vacuum pump, can be bought complete, with no need for a DIY set-up, which could be dangerous. (*See* Suppliers, page 156.) The equipment is very portable and takes up relatively little storage space, but it is expensive.

The principle behind this piece of equipment is amazingly simple. The ground and veneer are placed inside a strong bag from which the air is then extracted to create a vacuum. As this happens, the bag becomes compressed against the work, pressing the veneer against the ground using atmospheric pressure alone. Don't be sceptical about the effectiveness of this method because a large force is generated. Remember that atmospheric pressure is 15lb per square in (1kg per square cm). As an example, a surface 12in square (30cm square) would have the equivalent of 2,160lb (900kg) pressing down on it! Rather more than enough for the job.

SAND BOX

For occasional work, or where resources and space do not allow the use of a vacuum bag press, the sand box method is an adequate alternative. Before the advent of the vacuum press, the sand box was the traditional method for shaped veneering. The ground would be pressed into dry silver sand and removed, leaving behind an impression of the shape. The veneer was laid by placing ground and veneer into the sand and weighting it to maintain pressure. In restoration work where animal glue is used, the sand may be heated (*see* Chapter 5).

VENEER TAPE AND PINS

These may seem rather prosaic items compared with some of the more complex equipment described earlier in the chapter. Nevertheless, they are crucial.

Generally, there is a degree of moisture involved in the laying of veneers because of the glue. Where veneers are joined, they will need to be taped, mostly to ensure that their positions are maintained, but also to minimize the risk of the joints opening as the glue dries and the veneer shrinks slightly. Veneer tape is essentially gummed paper tape. It is easy to remove from the work later by moistening it to loosen it from the surface.

When constructing complex built-up veneer panels, the component parts are laid onto a drawn pattern prior to taping together. Veneer pins, which are very fine, are used to hold the pieces in position. Once taped up, the pins can be removed before laying the veneer onto the ground.

The pins are very thin, and so do not leave large and obvious holes later. Some pins have a plastic cap which makes them easier to push in by hand. Other varieties look like very thin moulding pins and can be used to secure veneers during laying when there is the danger of them slipping as the pressure is applied in a press (*see* Chapter 5).

Fig 3.20 A sand box press.

PREPARING VENEERS

♦ HANDLING AND STORING NEW VENEERS

♦ USING THE VENEER KNIFE

♦ DEALING WITH DEFECTS

♦ LENGTHENING A VENEER

♦ FLATTENING BUCKLED VENEERS

♦ COLOURING VENEERS

HANDLING AND STORING NEW VENEERS

Knife-cut veneers are fragile materials. This may not be so apparent when working with fairly small pieces, but with larger sheets that flex very easily, the prospect of causing serious damage to them is very real. Sawn veneers do not present this problem partly because of their thickness, but also because they are generally of a much smaller size.

When leaves of veneers are bought they will be supplied either flat or rolled, depending upon which method is easier for the purposes of carriage. To avoid undue risk of damage in transit large leaves can only be sent rolled, and will require some time to settle after unpacking. Allow time for the veneer to flatten gradually of its own accord, although some help may be required, by weighing down the ends with books. At first, do not put the books directly over the ends, as this may cause the veneer

to split, but place them at the point where the veneer begins to curl, and gradually slide them towards the end over a period of a day.

Smaller sheets of veneer may be supplied flat and will require less preparation for storage. Taping the ends is all that is likely to be required.

Before all this is done though, it is a good idea to tape the ends of all sheets of veneers as the ends are especially vulnerable to splits, and once established, these splits have a tendency to progress along the veneer's length. Taping with masking or veneer tape will reduce this risk, or at least minimize the extent of the migration. (*See* Fig 4.1.)

Once all new veneers have been allowed to settle and flatten, they should be stored horizontally and maintained in a flat position in a cool, dark, dry place. Flatness in storage is vital because any flexing in the search for a piece will weaken the veneer over a period of time, encouraging and nurturing splits and splintering. This risk increases with the age of the veneer, as it becomes more brittle over time. Store veneers off the ground and on a sheet

Fig 4.1 Taping the ends of a leaf of veneer will reduce the risk of splits appearing and worsening.

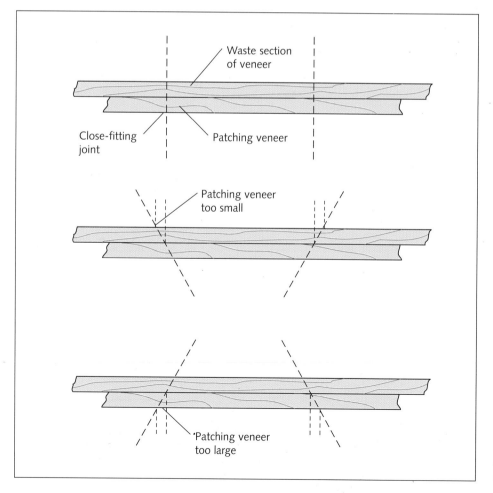

Fig 4.2 Cutting angle for the veneer knife.

Fig 4.3 There is a high risk of the veneer splintering out at the edge when cutting across the grain.

of chipboard or other flat board. Cover them to keep them clean and to exclude the light, because veneers suffer the same fate as solid wood, in changing colour after long-term exposure to light.

USING THE VENEER KNIFE

Much of the success achieved in veneering is down to the skill with which the veneer knife is used. Some of the techniques required are not easy at first, but become so with practice. The critical factor is the knife, and it is important that good cutting practice is adopted from the start.

When cutting the veneer, always ensure that the knife is held vertically. The blade will tend to compress the veneer on each side, but the fibres will relax and swell again with the glue during laying. If the knife is held off the vertical, there is the risk that the joints will be poorly fitting, as the shapes cut from the damaged and patching veneers will not match. (*See* Fig 4.2.)

CUTTING VENEER TO SIZE

Cutting veneer to the size appropriate for the job in hand may sound a simple task, and there is nothing especially complicated about it, but there are a couple of things that are worth bearing in mind. The thing to remember is that when you cut

across the grain, the veneer is likely to splinter, as shown in Fig 4.3. There are two things you can do to avoid the frustration of ruining a good piece of veneer. First, make the veneer oversize by about $^3/_8$in (10mm) all round. Second, when cutting to size, make the first cuts across the grain, and the final cutting to size along the grain so that the splintered edge can be cut away (*see* Fig 4.4).

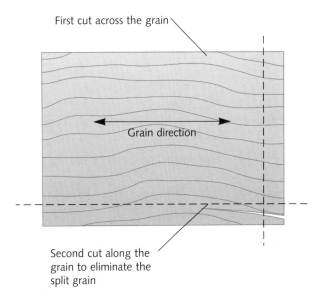

First cut across the grain

Grain direction

Second cut along the grain to eliminate the split grain

Fig 4.4 When cutting veneer to size, make the initial cuts across the grain. When you cut along the grain to produce the final size, the splintered edge will be cut away.

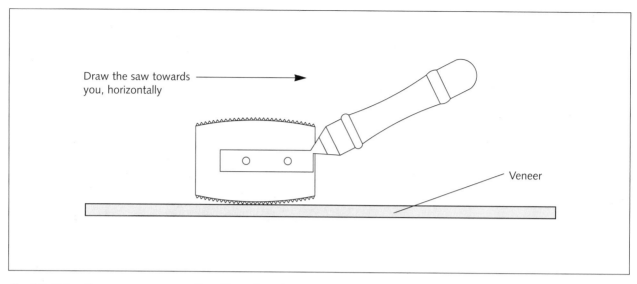

Fig 4.5 Using the veneer saw correctly will create a clean cutting action, without digging in.

VENEER SAW

You can use a veneer saw as an alternative to the veneer knife for cutting to size. It is especially useful for hard and brittle veneers, or sawn veneers, which would be difficult to cut with the knife. It is used with the straightedge in exactly the same way as the knife. Draw the saw towards you against the straightedge. The curve of the blade prevents it digging into the veneer. You do not need to apply pressure as you do with the knife. Figure 4.5 shows the action of the saw. Work across the grain before working along it, just as you would with the knife.

DEALING WITH DEFECTS

As it is a natural material, veneer does not necessarily come free of defects. In fact, one should expect to see, and to have to deal with, some minor ones. The two most commonly occurring problems are splits and holes.

SPLITS

Splits in the edge of a veneer are a serious problem as even small splits will gradually creep along the length of the veneer. If they are not dealt with, a veneer can eventually be rendered useless for laying as a complete leaf because it starts to break up.

Splits are also quite commonly found in the body of the veneer. These may be caused by rough handling, or be a consequence of age and increasing brittleness. Tape the split to hold the edges together and to prevent it worsening (see Fig 4.6). Note that the tape is applied across the split as well as along it. This will help hold the edges together, especially as the glue dries after laying, and the tape can be easily removed after laying the veneer (see Chapter 5). Don't remove it before laying – the edges of the split may open up as the veneer shrinks during the drying period.

Fig 4.6 Splits in a veneer must be taped to hold the edges together and to prevent the split from worsening.

Fig 4.7 Burr veneers (elm in this case) are prone to naturally occurring holes.

HOLES

In most cases, to make it virtually indistinguishable from the original, holes in the body of a veneer will need to be patched using a veneer of the same species, and as close to the damaged veneer in colour and figure as possible.

Figure 4.7 shows a hole in burr elm, a very common defect in this species. Burr elm and walnut are good examples of the problem of making patches 'invisible'. The wild figure makes it near impossible to make a completely invisible patch – a reasonable match is the best you can hope for here.

Figure 4.8 shows a variety of patches for different types of blemish. The dotted lines show the cuts that can be made and which follow, to a greater or lesser extent, the grain direction. If the veneer is selected well for figure and colour, and cut accurately using the natural contours of the veneer's figure as a guide, the patch will pass cursory inspection.

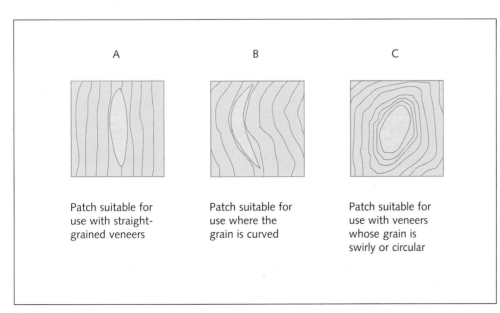

A

Patch suitable for use with straight-grained veneers

B

Patch suitable for use where the grain is curved

C

Patch suitable for use with veneers whose grain is swirly or circular

Fig 4.8 Patches should be cut so that they follow the general figure direction wherever possible.

VENEERING ~ A COMPLETE COURSE

PATCHING A HOLE

1 Place the damaged veneer over the patching veneer. This allows the patching veneer to be viewed through the hole. Both veneers must be perfectly flat. Burr veneers tend to be buckled and will need to be flattened beforehand (*see* page 47).

2 Move the damaged piece over the patching piece to find the best match for colour and figure. Where the hole is long and narrow, it can be difficult to view the veneer beneath in order to gain a good match. If this is the case, it may be worth making the hole a little larger by cutting around it to create a larger viewing 'window'. A balance must be struck though, between creating a good match and making the patch larger than it needs to be.

3 The patch is produced by cutting through both pieces of veneer. The best results are obtained using a single cut: if you need to make a second or third cut, you run the risk of making the joint much more obvious. If necessary, use veneer pins to secure the two veneers while you cut the patch out. Keep the veneer knife vertical at all times to ensure that the patch is the same size as the hole cut to receive it. (*See* Chapter 3, pages 26-7.) As a general rule, avoid cutting directly across the grain – it is virtually impossible to make such a cut invisible. Ideally, the cut should closely follow the direction of the figure, though in practice, you may need to compromise. There will almost certainly be a need to cut across the grain at some point, and this is best done by cutting diagonally across it. The shape of the patch is determined by the nature of the damage, but follow the direction of the figure as far as possible so that it is not obvious.

4 Remove the waste veneer from the damaged veneer, and fit the patch in its place. Secure it with veneer tape or rub a little PVA glue into the joint on the reverse side, and allow to dry. Keep the tape in place during laying, only removing it when cleaning up the work afterwards. This means that you will need to plan the work carefully: if you are book-matching or quartering, it is very easy to end up with the taped side of the patch actually facing down onto the groundwork when you open out the veneer pack. (*See* Chapter 7.)

LENGTHENING A VENEER

While it is possible to lengthen a strip of veneer by joining a second piece to it, end-to-end, there will be an obvious discontinuity across the joint. There may be occasions when you want the join to be invisible, or at least nearly so, for example, where a veneer is being applied to a wide circumference, such as the frieze of a table top, and you want to create the impression of a continuous piece of veneer. To achieve this, the technique to use is finger joints (*see* Figs 4.9 to 4.13). The best results are obtained where veneers of a close match for colour and figure direction can be used.

TO LENGTHEN VENEER

1 Overlap the two veneers to be joined by a substantial amount (*see* Fig 4.9). The longer you cut the fingers, the more likely it is that the joint will be invisible, but the greater the wastage incurred.

2 Tape the overlap so that the veneers will not slip while cutting and, if you wish, use veneer pins to stabilize both veneers.

3 Draw two parallel lines on the top veneer with a pencil (*see* Fig 4.10). The fingers will be cut between these lines. Note that the two lines must fall within the overlapping sections of veneer. Mark out equal distances on both lines. Each marked position represents the point of one of the fingers. The closer the spacing, the more invisible the joint, because the cuts will be closer to the direction of the figure. However, this does increase the amount of work involved, the increased risk of error, and the possible weakness of the fingers because they are so slender. It is not essential to mark out the fingers themselves because an invisible joint does not depend on uniformity, only accuracy, but for reassurance, you can mark out the fingers with a pencil and straightedge (*see* Fig 4.11).

4 Cut the fingers, using the straightedge as a guide (*see* Fig 4.12). It is important to overcut the parallel lines by a fraction. This is to ensure that the cut is complete at the point of each finger. It

Fig 4.9 Lengthening a piece of veneer. Match the colour and figure of the two veneers as closely as possible.

Fig 4.10 Draw two parallel lines and mark out equal distances: these mark the points of the fingers.

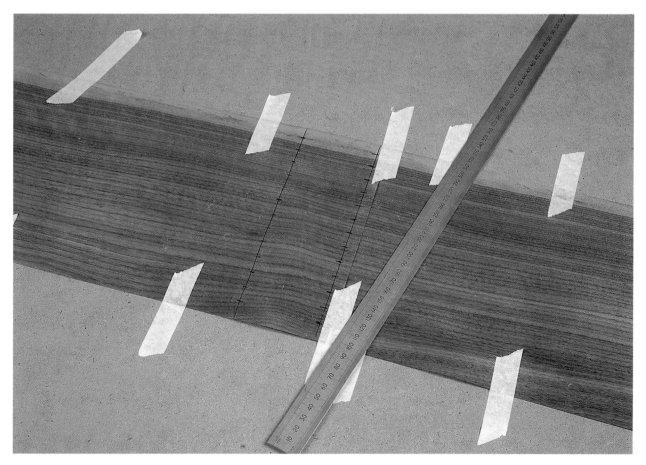

Fig 4.11 Marking out the fingers is optional, but it does give extra confidence if you are inexperienced.

Fig 4.12 Using a straight edge and very sharp veneer knife, cut the fingers. It is essential that you cut through both pieces of veneer with one cut.

would be a disaster if, after cutting all the fingers, you discovered that the pieces of waste veneer would not separate from the fingers because they weren't completely severed.

Figure 4.13 shows a completed finger joint. If possible, use a species, such as sycamore, that is relatively easy to match up. When laid and sanded, the joint will pass cursory inspection. Once the joint has been cut, and the fingers interlocked after removing the waste veneers, you will need to tape the joints to keep them close. The tape has been applied to the underside in Fig 4.13 so that the

Fig 4.13 The completed finger joint.

joint could be photographed: in practice, it is the upper side that should be taped. You can see a faint line on a couple of the joints in the photo. These are the pencil lines drawn earlier. They will disappear on sanding, but it is a good example of why it is better to cut the fingers without drawing them in.

FLATTENING BUCKLED VENEERS

Some of the very highly decorative veneers, such as burrs and curls, buckle easily. While this does not present a problem in terms of the quality of the veneer itself, many of the techniques used to prepare, shape and lay the veneer become impractical because they will not lie flat enough. Thus, before working with buckled veneers, it is necessary to flatten them. This is different from flattening veneer that has been supplied rolled: rolled veneer will curl in one plane only (i.e. along its length), while buckled veneer will undulate in several directions (*see* Fig 4.14). If veneers are to be joined, it is essential that they are completely flat, otherwise a good joint cannot be obtained. Buckled veneers will also encourage the pooling of glue during the pressing process, resulting in small, hard lumps in the work.

To flatten the veneer, moisten it well with warm water to make it pliable, place it between plain white paper or blotting paper, and then apply pressure – you can use a veneer press, or cauls. Leave overnight to dry out before releasing the veneer and inspecting it. At the very least, the veneers should be considerably flatter, but if they are still not flat enough to work with, repeat the process.

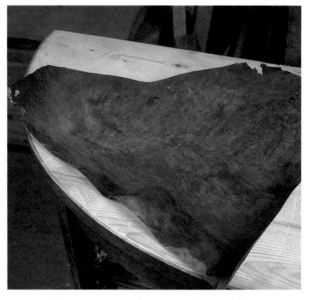

Fig 4.14 This buckled piece of burr walnut needs to be flattened before it can be laid.

COLOURING VENEERS

You can use contrasting colour as well as figure to create a decorative impact. In particular, marquetry and some parquetry effects rely upon a range of colour combinations and contrasts. While there are sufficient variations in the natural colour of veneers, because of the range of species available, artificially coloured veneers can be used as well. Indeed, there are many fine examples of veneered work where a variety of 'non-natural' colours have been used. The work of the Art Nouveau movement included the use of artificially coloured veneers to represent such things as flowers. Much contemporary work has also benefited from the availability of reliable, light-fast dyes.

There is little difficulty in staining veneers after laying, provided you are dealing with a single species and there are no colour contrasts to be preserved. Where contrasts of colour need to be retained, such as in marquetry work, staining after laying does present a problem. In such circumstances, it is best to stain the veneer prior to laying.

Colouring materials fall into two main types: those that dye the wood and those that change its colour through chemical action. The former are easier to use in that the colour change is predictable – the natural colour of the wood will have some effect, but the final colour will, broadly, be that of the colouring material. Chemical stains are less predictable because they depend upon the chemical make-up of the particular wood, and the final colour of the wood is markedly different from that of the stain itself.

DYEING THE VENEER

The most effective way of achieving a uniform colour that penetrates to the full thickness of the veneer (to allow for light sanding when finishing and polishing) is to immerse it in a container of the dye for a couple of hours. Water-based aniline dyes are very effective, as the water-borne dye penetrates the wood fibres very easily.

After removing the veneer from the dye bath, remove the surplus dye from the surface and allow the veneer to dry in a warm place. The veneer will tend to curl as a result of the dyeing process, and it will need to be flattened before laying, as for a buckled veneer (*see* page 47).

PROPRIETARY WOOD DYES

There are many proprietary brands of wood dye on the market. They are reliable colouring materials, but the range of colours tends to be limited, with each brand name having its own colour palette. Well-known brand names include Colron, Blackfriar's, Rustins, and Liberon.

ANILINE DYES

Some very dramatic – even startling – effects can be achieved using these dyes. They are available in a very wide range of colours, including 'natural' wood shades and 'pure' colours, providing an opportunity to experiment with a huge number of combinations. They are very strong colouring agents and need to be used with some caution to prevent the colour overpowering the veneer. Where striking colours are being used, as in Fig 4.15, it is usual to use light coloured veneers, such as sycamore. In fact, the grey veneer has been coloured with grey aniline dye and simulates harewood. Harewood was traditionally produced by immersing sycamore in a solution of iron sulphate, which causes a chemical reaction that turns sycamore grey. It is more usual these days to use aniline dye to produce harewood.

Aniline dyes come in two forms: water- and alcohol-soluble. They can be bought in powder form, to be made up with the appropriate solvent (i.e. water or methylated spirit respectively), or in the ready-made concentrated liquid form.

CHEMICAL STAINING AGENTS

A number of chemicals will change the colour of some woods. The exact nature of this effect depends upon the susceptibility of individual species and, of course, the materials to which they are susceptible. The most common staining agents are described below, along with the effects they create. With the exception of fuming with ammonia, the chemical stains are applied by immersion, similar to that described above.

The difficulty with chemical stains is that they are unpredictable. So much depends on the chemical nature of the veneer itself, and two pieces of the same species may not even react in the same way. Aniline dyes and the proprietary wood dyes are much more reliable.

AMMONIA (FUMED OAK)

Ammonia is a particularly unpleasant material to work with. It is strongly alkaline, will irritate the sensitive membranes of the respiratory tract and eyes, and is corrosive if it comes into contact with skin. Ammonia is actually a gas, but is very highly soluble in water, and it is as a solution that you will buy it. The fumes given off by the solution is ammonia gas and many people will have been exposed to this at some time or other – an experience not to be repeated or forgotten!

As a liquid, ammonia has little effect on the colour of oak, but when exposed to the fumes it will gradually change colour through a range of shades, from honey to inky black. The process can be arrested at any time by removing

the oak veneer from the fumes. The veneer is placed in a clear container with a plastic dish of household ammonia (not metal as ammonia will attack the metal). The clear, sealed container allows the change in the veneer's colour to be observed safely.

IRON SULPHATE

This chemical is used to create harewood, a silvery, greyish variety of sycamore. Harewood can be bought ready-stained from veneer suppliers, but you may want to make your own, in which case you can soak the veneer in a solution of iron sulphate. To be frank, it is easier and more reliable to use grey aniline dye.

IRON ACETATE

Several nails left in vinegar overnight produces this very effective chemical agent. If oak is soaked in the resultant liquid it turns black!

Fig 4.15 These brightly coloured veneers have been produced by soaking sycamore veneer in water-soluble aniline dye.

5

LAYING VENEERS

- ◆ **PREPARING THE GROUNDWORK**
- ◆ **BALANCING AND COUNTER VENEERS**
- ◆ **PRINCIPAL VENEER LAYING METHODS**
- ◆ **CLEANING UP**
- ◆ **REPAIRING BLISTERS AND LIFTED EDGES**

PREPARING THE GROUNDWORK

A good bond between veneer and groundwork is ensured only if the groundwork is flat across its surface. Keying the surface (i.e. creating a slight roughness) enables the glue to get a 'hold' on the surface and thus encourages a good bond.

ACHIEVING A FLAT SURFACE

This is of less concern with MDF, ply and chipboard than it is with solid wood groundwork. Their means of manufacture generally ensures that they are flat across their whole surface. Solid wood, on the other hand, does not have such an advantage, and its flatness and freedom from problematic blemishes, such as planing tears (areas where wood grain has been torn out by the use of a plane), depends very much on the skill used and care taken in its preparation.

Any hollows may discourage adhesion, leading to the possibility of bubbles. This is particularly so with conventional flat presses that provide pressure on high spots, but very little on hollow areas. A solid groundwork must be tested for flatness across the whole surface, using a straightedge. Two straightedges can be used as sights to ensure that the groundwork is not twisted (*see* Fig 5.1).

Planing tears and other blemishes of this nature need to be filled with a proprietary filler and then smoothed prior to keying, and it is important that knots are removed and patched (*see* Chapter 2, page 16). There may be no immediate difficulty in laying a veneer over a knot, but over a period of time the shape of the knot usually shows through as the ground shrinks a little, leaving the knot proud of the surface.

KEYING OR 'TOOTHING' THE GROUND

A slight roughness to a surface aids the ability of an adhesive to do its job. This was perhaps more important in the past than it is now because of the nature of modern glues. Nevertheless, it is still good practice to slightly roughen the groundwork prior to laying.

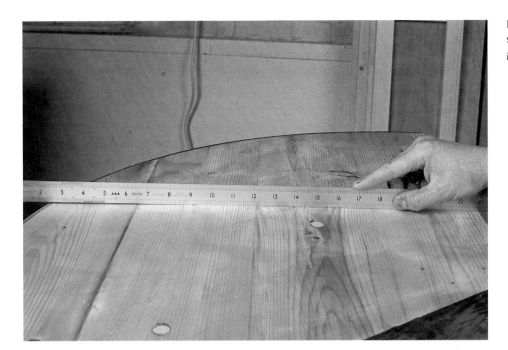

Fig 5.1 Using straightedges to test groundwork for flatness.

Fig 5.2 A toothing plane must be worked randomly over the entire groundwork to remove blemishes and possible high spots.

The traditional way of applying a key on a solid wood groundwork is by using a toothing plane (*see* Chapter 3). This can be held in one hand and worked randomly over the whole surface (*see* Fig 5.2). Its vertically positioned blade has a very finely serrated cutting edge that scores the surface. This has two effects. Firstly, the fine grooves it produces on the surface provide a key for the glue. Secondly, the sole of the plane will ride over high spots, levelling them out. Work the toothing plane over the surface to generate the key and even out undulations. Continue until the whole surface is covered with the grooves. If, after this treatment, you are able to see areas not toothed, these are low spots, and further toothing will be needed or the surface planed flat and then worked again. Always work the whole surface to ensure uniformity. If you dwell on any one area, a hollow is likely to result. Wipe away the dust afterwards.

Manufactured boards, such as MDF and ply, should not require the use of a toothing plane, because their surfaces are flat. In most cases, manufactured boards need little more than a good scouring with coarse abrasive paper, though if there are holes or dents they will need to be filled and smoothed as with solid wood. After scouring, wipe the surface clear of dust.

Remember, both sides of the groundwork will need to be toothed if the back is being veneered as well.

SIZING THE GROUNDWORK

If you plan to use water-based adhesives (such as animal glue or PVA), it is a good idea to size the groundwork first to prevent premature drying as water is absorbed from the adhesive into the surface of the groundwork. Sizing will reduce the absorption.

There are several ways to size the surface. The easiest way is to brush thinned glue over the surface and allow it to dry thoroughly before continuing with the veneer laying. If you use PVA glue as the size, thin it down in the ratio of one part glue to five parts water. Use a similar ratio if

you use pearl glue. A very good alternative is decorators' size (available from good decorators' suppliers). Follow the maker's mixing instructions.

BALANCING AND COUNTER VENEERS

BALANCING VENEER

A veneer has the ability to distort the groundwork. To minimize the risk of this, veneer should be laid on the heartwood side (*see* Chapter 2). Better still, wide surfaces should be made up of several narrow boards butt jointed (*see* Fig 2.17, page 15). However, even this may not be sufficient to eliminate the ability of a veneer to distort the groundwork! When water-based adhesives are used, a veneer will swell. Consequently, as the veneer dries, it will begin to shrink imperceptibly and the force with which it does so is surprisingly strong – enough to cause the ground to bend a little under the stress (*see* Fig 5.3), especially if the groundwork is relatively thin and wide. Hammer veneering can increase this effect because the process can stretch the veneer a little. Stretching the veneer during laying should be avoided because it will shrink as the glue dries and increase the amount of pull.

Distortion can be prevented by laying a veneer of the same species on the reverse of the ground. This *balancing veneer*, as it is called, must be laid at the same time as the main, or show, veneer: you cannot reverse any distortion by adding the balancing veneer later. As the show veneer pulls on

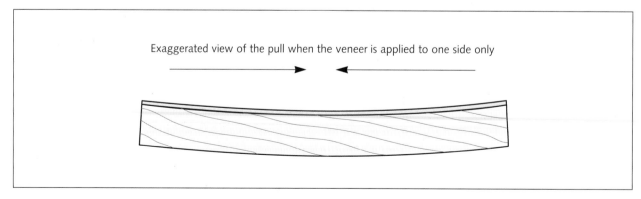

Exaggerated view of the pull when the veneer is applied to one side only

Fig 5.3 A wide veneer can exert a pull on the groundwork. Stretching the veneer during laying should be avoided because it will shrink as the glue dries and increase the amount of pull.

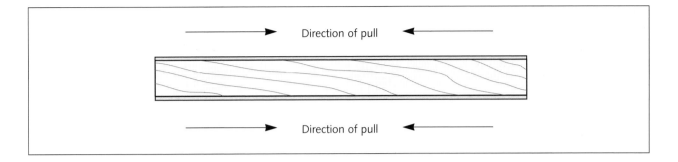

Fig 5.4 A balancing veneer will create an opposing pull to the show veneer, thereby neutralizing the effect.

one side of the wood, the balancing veneer will do the same thing on the other side, neutralizing the distorting effect (*see* Fig 5.4).

COUNTER VENEER

All groundwork should have a balancing veneer, but where solid wood makes up the groundwork, and the work is to be of the highest quality, then *counter veneering* should also be carried out. Counter veneering creates, in effect, a two-layered ply on both sides of the ground. The counter veneers

should be of the same, or similar, species as the show veneer, but laid at right angles to the direction of the grain of the groundwork (*see* Fig 5.5). The balancing and show veneers are then laid on top of this, with their grain at right angles to the counter veneers (i.e. in the same direction as the ground). The purpose of counter veneering is to minimize the effects caused by the movement of solid wood.

It is generally unnecessary to counter veneer MDF and chipboard, because they do not suffer from the potential difficulties of solid wood (*see*

Fig 5.5 Counter veneers are laid with the grain direction at right angles to that of the show and balancing veneers.

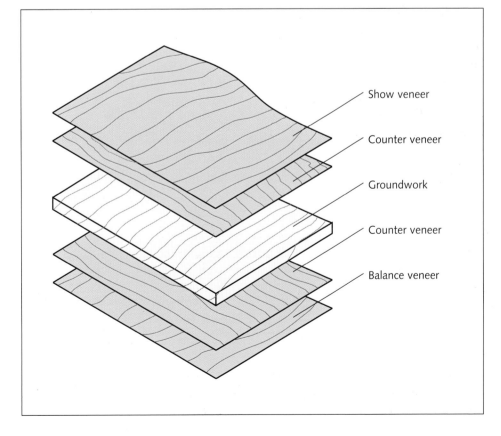

Show veneer

Counter veneer

Groundwork

Counter veneer

Balance veneer

Chapter 2). Plywood, blockboard and laminboard should be counter veneered if you are unable to lay the show veneer at right angles to the grain direction of the board's surface (*see* Chapter 2, page 17). Some cheaper chipboards do have a roughish surface that will show through the veneer after a period of settling down, and it is worth counter veneering to prevent this.

OVERVIEW OF LAYING VENEERS

A general principle of veneering is, follow the same operations on both sides of the groundwork, to balance any possible detrimental effects, and do it to both sides at the same time. The order of steps in preparing the groundwork is:

1 Key the surfaces (both sides if counter and/or balancing veneers are being used).

2 Lay counter veneers to both sides as a single operation, if these are being used.

3 Lay the show veneer and balancing veneer as a single operation, after the counter veneers, if these have been used.

4 Trim off excess veneer and clean up the work after the glue has had time to set.

As a general rule of thumb, when laying veneers with a press, leave the work in the press for as long as is practicable. Leaving overnight should be the norm. For industrial workshops, this is a problem because of the reduction in the production rate,

and for this reason commercial presses are frequently heated to accelerate the setting of the glue. However, for the small workshop, and the amateur woodworker, the schedule needs to be planned to allow the work to be left undisturbed in the press. The caul press, in particular, may cause you some difficulty because of the number of clamps that will be needed, so you need to bear this in mind.

The methods of laying veneer are explained in detail first, with methods of cleaning up and trimming excess veneer explained towards the end of the chapter. Cleaning up the work should not be seen as some distinct and separate activity from the process of laying the veneer – I have explained the processes separately for the sake of clarity.

EDGING MANUFACTURED BOARDS

Veneering the surface of any of the manufactured boards leaves the edges exposed, making it obvious that the veneer has been laid over it. These exposed edges need to be disguised with some form of edging. The simplest, but most vulnerable to damage and lifting, would be veneer glued along the edge. There are better and more secure means of edging the groundwork.

A solid wood edging may be pinned or glued to the edge before the veneer is laid (*see* Fig 5.6). This is usually the same species as the veneer to give the

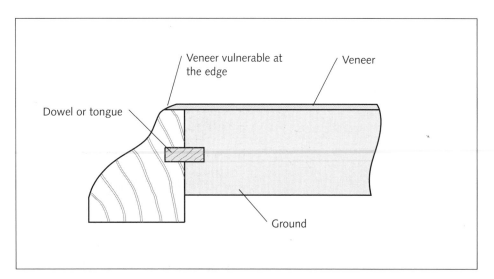

Fig 5.6 **An edging can be glued, pinned, dowelled or tongued into the groundwork.**

Veneer vulnerable at the edge

Veneer

Dowel or tongue

Ground

Fig 5.7 Adding an edge moulding after laying the veneer offers better protection for the veneer's edge.

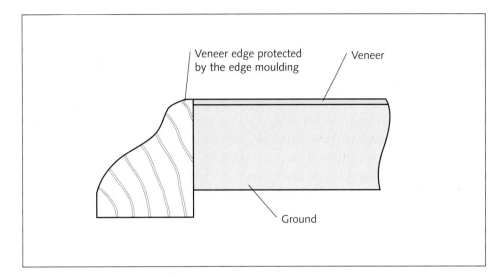

Veneer edge protected by the edge moulding

Veneer

Ground

impression of solid wood. The difficulty with this is that the edge of the veneer itself remains vulnerable. Figure 5.7 shows how this can be overcome: the veneer can be laid first and the edge moulding added afterwards. This protects the edge of the veneer, but it is obvious that the work is veneered. Considerable care is needed because the edging must remain flush with the veneered surface and this may require some light planing with a smoothing plane. The big danger is that you may plane through the veneer to the groundwork beneath. I find that it is best to set the plane for an extremely fine cut (i.e. the shaving is translucent and as thin as the brown outer skin of an onion). Plane the surplus from the edging with a slicing action, working from the veneered side outwards (*see* Fig 5.8).

Alternatively, for thicker groundwork, the edging could be fitted with dowels or a tongue and groove. With these the veneer will reach the very edge, giving the impression of a completely solid board. The difficulty here is that the edge of the veneer is left vulnerable. Edges are particularly difficult and if any part of the veneer hasn't bonded properly, it is often here. This can be caused by surplus glue oozing out and lifting the edge.

An alternative method is to mould the edge with a router after the veneer has been laid. The effect of this is to make the veneer feather into the moulding so that they look as one (*see* Fig 5.9). This method is ideal where the edge needs to have a heavily moulded shape.

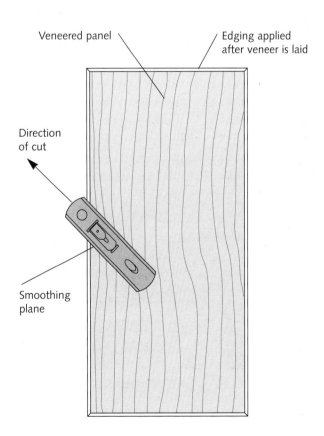

Veneered panel

Edging applied after veneer is laid

Direction of cut

Smoothing plane

Fig 5.8 The edge may stand proud of the groundwork's surface. Plane the surplus with a very finely set smoothing plane, using a slicing action working towards the edge.

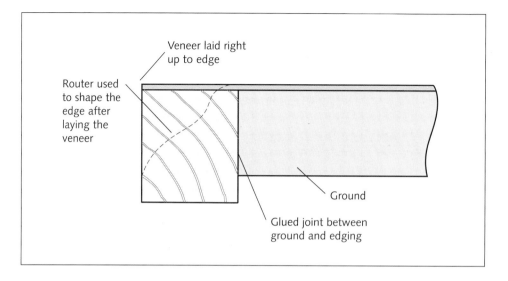

Fig 5.9 For shaped mouldings of the edge, it is better to fit the edging unshaped, and create the moulding with a router, after laying.

Veneer laid right up to edge

Router used to shape the edge after laying the veneer

Ground

Glued joint between ground and edging

PRINCIPAL VENEER LAYING METHODS

USING GLUE FILM

Glue films are suitable for laying single sheets of veneer on flat surfaces. There are two ways of laying veneer with glue film, both of which can be achieved using the minimum of equipment.

METHOD 1

1 Prepare the groundwork and veneer (for advice *see* pages 50–4).

2 Cut a piece of glue film slightly larger than the groundwork.

3 Place the shiny (glued) side of the paper onto the groundwork and run a warm iron over the whole surface to melt and transfer the glue from the paper to the groundwork (*see* Fig 5.10). The heat setting of the iron should be that for silk (i.e. the middle heat setting). Use some pressure and move the iron slowly over the paper.

4 Carefully peel off the backing paper after it has cooled – the glue will remain bonded to the groundwork. Keep the paper for placing over the veneer as you iron it onto the groundwork.

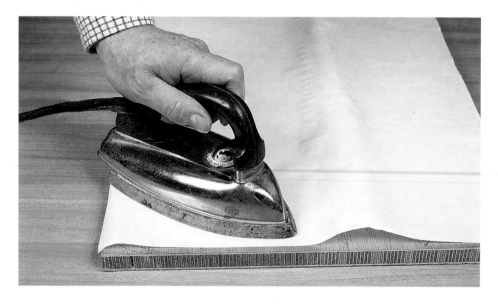

Fig 5.10 Transferring the glue from glue film to the groundwork. The iron is moved slowly over the paper backing to ensure that the glue melts.

Fig 5.11 As the iron melts the glue, use a veneer hammer to press the veneer down, applying pressure from the centre out.

5 Cut the veneer slightly oversize to allow for trimming and cleaning up afterwards.

6 Lay the veneer over the glued surface and moisten it slightly to keep it pliable, and to prevent the veneer shrinking as it is heated with the iron.

7 Place the glue film backing paper over the veneer and, working from the centre outwards, slowly run the iron over it, using some pressure, to remove the air and ensure good contact with the glue. It is important to work slowly to ensure that the glue melts, and to work outwards from the centre to ensure that air is not trapped beneath the veneer. The heat setting should be the same as before. To improve bonding, use the veneer hammer to rub the veneer down as the iron moves over the surface (see Fig 5.11). The hammer can be held in a variety of ways, depending on the preference of the worker. This is my preferred method as it allows considerable pressure to be exerted.

8 Clean up and trim the veneer (see page 72).

METHOD 2

1 Prepare the groundwork and veneer (see pages 39–52). Cut a piece of glue film slightly larger than the groundwork.

2 Carefully peel the film of glue from the backing paper, keeping it intact.

3 Place this film over the groundwork, removing any wrinkles so that it lies flat.

4 Lay the veneer, cut slightly oversize to allow for trimming and cleaning up, over the film of glue and moisten it slightly.

5 Iron the veneer down onto the groundwork, covering the whole surface, working slowly from the centre outwards. The iron should be on the middle heat setting, as for silk. As the iron moves over the surface, rub the veneer down with the veneer hammer, to improve bonding.

6 Clean up and trim the veneer (see page 72).

USING CONTACT ADHESIVES

Contact adhesives are a convenient way of laying a single sheet of veneer over a flat or shaped surface. No heat is required, but there is no room for error. Both the groundwork and veneer are coated with adhesive (see Fig 5.12), which is spread evenly, using a serrated spreader (usually supplied with the adhesive). The glue must be left to dry for about 15 minutes (depending on the instructions that accompany it) before laying the veneer. When the two glued surfaces come into contact with each other, they will bond immediately (hence the term 'contact' adhesive). This can cause problems if you do not position the veneer absolutely correctly at the first attempt, which is difficult if you are laying a large sheet of veneer. To overcome this potential difficulty, the method to adopt is called the 'slip sheet' method. In this, a piece of thick, smooth paper, such as brown parcel paper, is placed over the groundwork, without applying any pressure. The veneer is then gently laid over the paper and positioned carefully, again without applying even the slightest amount of pressure. The paper forms a

Fig 5.12 Spread a thin, even coat of contact adhesive over the veneer and the groundwork. A serrated spreader is provided with the adhesive.

barrier between the two glued surfaces. When you are satisfied that the veneer is positioned correctly, you can start to gently slip the paper out, rubbing down the veneer onto the groundwork with a veneer hammer or roller as you do so (*see* Fig 5.13).

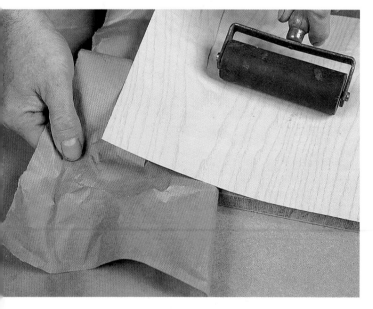

Fig 5.13 The slip method prevents premature bonding of the veneer to the ground, giving much more control over the process.

HAMMER VENEERING

The term 'hammer' is something of a misnomer for this method of laying veneers. The veneer hammer is used to press the veneer against the groundwork. In hammer veneering, pearl glue is used, as its ability to 'grab' the veneer makes it unnecessary to use a press. The technique cannot be used with other adhesives, although, as described above, you can use a hammer to rub down a veneer when using a contact adhesive or glue film. However, there you are laying veneer as a single sheet – it is impractical to make joints between adjacent veneers using these adhesives. Pearl glue allows you to make joints (*see* page 61), because the glue can be re-heated as required while you work.

PROBLEMS WITH HAMMER VENEERING

There are several errors to be avoided when using this method of laying veneers:

● Excess glue can make the work a little lumpy, so it will need to be squeezed out.

● Stretching the veneer during laying is something that ought to be avoided. Stretched veneer has a tendency to shrink again as it dries out, and this can cause joints between veneers to open. If too much glue is used, you run the risk of stretching the veneer in the attempt to squeeze out any surplus.

● The consistency of the glue is critical (*see* Chapter 2, pages 20–1). If it has too thick a consistency, it is difficult to spread a thin layer over the ground and, if you do need to 'hammer' out surplus glue, it does not flow quite so easily, so there is a greater risk of stretching the veneer as more force is applied.

After reading what to avoid, you may have the impression that this method is fraught with difficulty, but that is not the case. Hammer veneering is an easy method to master and has a number of positive advantages. No special equipment is necessary, and you have the advantage of viewing the work as it progresses. With a veneer press of any description, once the work is placed in the equipment it remains hidden from view until it is removed. Occasionally, the veneer can slip as pressure is applied (although there are ways to minimize this risk), but when using the hammer, you can build up fairly complex patterns, such as quartering and cross-banding (*see* Chapters 6 and 7), and you are able to correct mistakes as you go along.

Readers familiar with pearl glue may be conscious that there is generally a need to work quite quickly, as the glue gels rapidly. In this method of veneering, the gelling is an advantage because rather than you being forced to work quickly, hammer veneering allows you to take your time. There is no need to rush! Pearl glue can only bond when surfaces are brought into contact while the glue is hot and fluid. When veneering, it is often necessary to spend time positioning the veneer before making the bond. Allowing the glue to chill and gel allows you to place the veneers onto the groundwork without fear of premature bonding.

Where there is a need to join veneers, either for a decorative effect or for the more practical reason of covering an area wider than the veneer itself, this is done during the laying process (*see* page 61). You cannot pre-joint veneers prior to hammer laying.

LAYING A SINGLE SHEET OF VENEER

1 Spread a thin, even layer of glue over the prepared ground (*see* pages 20–1 and Fig 5.14). The glue will gel fairly quickly, but this does not matter. In fact, it can be an advantage to let the glue set before placing the veneer on the ground because it allows you to move it over the surface to ensure perfect placement. The glue will be re-heated and liquefied with a clothes iron when it is time to lay the veneer.

2 Position the veneer, which should have been prepared and cut to shape and size with a small overlap to allow for trimming (*see* Chapter 4, page 40), on the groundwork *after the glue has cooled and gelled*. The veneer will not stick to the cold glue, so you can reposition it if necessary. Ensure that there is a slight overlap all round the groundwork.

3 Lightly moisten the surface of the veneer to make it more pliable, and place a sheet of clean brown wrapping paper over the veneer. The purpose of the paper is to form a protective barrier between the veneer and the iron used to heat and melt the glue. The paper also makes it easier for the iron to slide over the surface.

4 Pre-heat the iron to its medium setting, and work it slowly over the surface of the brown paper so that the heat melts the glue on the groundwork. (*See* Fig 5.15.)

5 After heating the veneer and glue, remove the paper and use the veneer hammer to press down the veneer while the glue is still warm and liquid. If the piece is fairly large, this is best done in sections. It is difficult to define what is large because this will depend on the worker's preference and skill: the key question is, how large an area are you able to lay while the glue remains warm and liquid? When the iron is removed, the glue will remain liquid for only a limited period, and the veneer will not stick to the ground if the glue cools and sets again. This is why the process is more manageable if it is worked

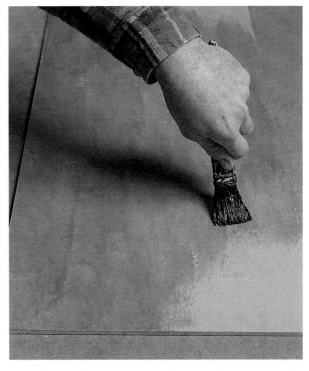

Fig 5.14 Brush a thin layer of glue over the groundwork and allow it to cool and gel.

Fig 5.15 A sheet of paper between the veneer and iron protects the iron from contamination, and at the same time reduces the friction on the sole of the iron.

Fig 5.16 Use the veneer hammer to press the veneer down onto the groundwork.

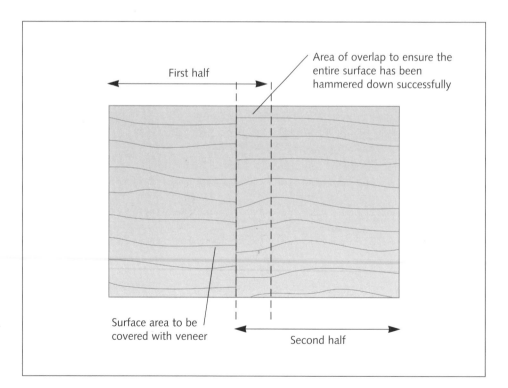

First half

Area of overlap to ensure the entire surface has been hammered down successfully

Surface area to be covered with veneer

Second half

Fig 5.17 Larger surfaces can be tackled in two halves. Note the area of overlap to make sure that no area is missed out.

The area is divided into quadrants, each being tackled in turn

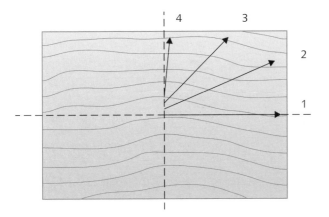

Fig 5.18 Working the veneer hammer over the surface. The numbers show the order of the strokes.

in sections. (*See* Fig 5.17.) To press down the veneer, press the brass strip against the veneer surface and stroke the veneer from the centre outwards. (*See* Figs 5.16 and 5.18.) Use sufficient pressure to force out any air bubbles and glue pockets, and press down any curled edges, but not so much as to crease or stretch the veneer. Take care at the edges: the hammer should be held diagonally to ensure that while pressure is applied here, the hammer does not fall off and damage the veneer. (*See* Fig 5.19.) If you have divided the work into sections, treat each section separately, heating and rubbing down one at a time.

6 Stubborn edges or bubbles can be treated by local re-heating and rubbing down. If you have used the correct amount of glue, only a small amount will have oozed out at the edges.

7 Clean up and trim the veneer (*see* page 72). If you have used too much glue you can remove some of the excess that oozes out from the edge to make cleaning up somewhat easier later. You will need to wait awhile until the glue has gelled very firmly, at which time you can literally peel it away from the edge with a small chisel or knife. However, take care not to damage the veneer.

MAKING A JOINT

On occasion, there may be a need to increase the width of a veneer by joining two or more sheets. This may be necessary to cover a groundwork that is too wide for one sheet, or for a decorative effect, such as book-matching (*see* Chapter 7).

1 Draw a line on the groundwork to mark the position of the joint. In most cases this will be at the centre of the groundwork if two veneers are being joined (*see* Fig 5.20). If more than one joint is needed, position them at equal distances from each other. For example, if three sheets of veneer are used, divide the groundwork into thirds and draw the two joint lines.

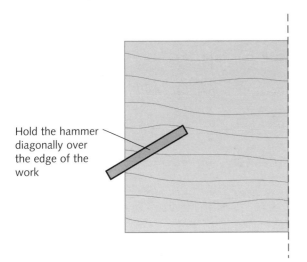

Hold the hammer diagonally over the edge of the work

Fig 5.19 Placement of hammer for pressing down veneer at the edges of work.

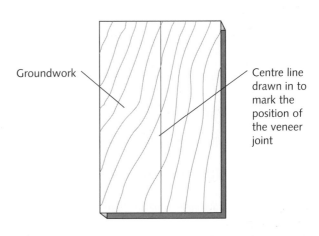

Groundwork

Centre line drawn in to mark the position of the veneer joint

Fig 5.20 Marking the position of a veneer joint on the groundwork.

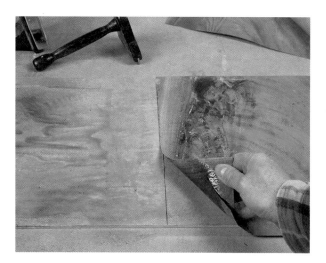

Fig 5.21 The first piece of veneer is laid as before so that the internal edge overlaps the line drawn to mark the join.

2 Apply glue over the entire surface and lay the first sheet of veneer as for a single sheet, described above, with the edge of the veneer overlapping the drawn joint line (*see* Fig 5.21).

3 Place the second sheet on the groundwork so that it overlaps the first veneer at the joint line, and lay this sheet. Note, in Fig 5.22, that the overlapping area of veneer has been hammered down as well.

4 To make the joint, lay a straightedge at the centre of the overlap and hold it in place with small clamps. Use a veneer knife to cut through the overlapping veneers (*see* Fig 5.23). It is essential that this is done with one cut only as two or more cuts will increase the risk of producing an open joint. The veneer is damp because of the glue, so it is easy to cut through the two sheets.

Remove the straightedge, and carefully remove the top, waste veneer. The lower strip of veneer can then be removed by gently peeling back the top veneer and lifting out the waste, using a chisel or sharp blade to ease it off the ground (*see* Fig 5.24).

5 Finally, hammer the edges of the joint down and tape them to prevent the joint opening as the glue dries. (*See* Fig 5.25.) If you are working with a large area, it may be necessary to re-heat the glue at the joint before hammering down.

VENEERING SHAPED WORK

Simple shapes, for example, the rail of a curved table, can be veneered with the hammer. The natural ability of pearl glue to 'grab' the veneer enables the curve of the rail to be negotiated without any difficulty, including joining adjacent pieces of veneer.

Fig 5.22 The second veneer is laid so that its internal edge overlaps that of the first veneer *and* the line drawn making the joint.

Fig 5.23 A veneer knife and clamped straight edge are used to cut through the overlapping veneers to make the joint.

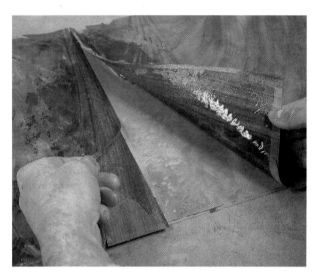

Fig 5.24 After removing the waste veneer from the top, lift the top veneer and remove the waste from underneath.

Fig 5.25 After removing the waste, iron the joint to re-heat the glue and hammer the edges down. Tape the joint to prevent it opening as the glue dries.

CAUL VENEERING

This is a very effective way of laying veneers on flat surfaces without expensive pressing equipment. The method can be set up for one-off work or for short production runs. The main difficulty is that caul veneering usually requires many clamps – a pair for each bearer – even for relatively small areas of work, though bolts can be substituted. The maxim that a workshop never has enough clamps is a truism for this type of work! You may need to buy or beg extra clamps. Plan your work before you lay the veneers: it is better to use more cauls than less to ensure uniformity of pressure across the whole surface. (*See* Chapter 3, page 36.)

Caul veneering can be used for any flat veneering project, including, with slight modifications, any of the built-up techniques described later in the book. The method allows for the use of most glues, and even for the use of heat to accelerate the setting

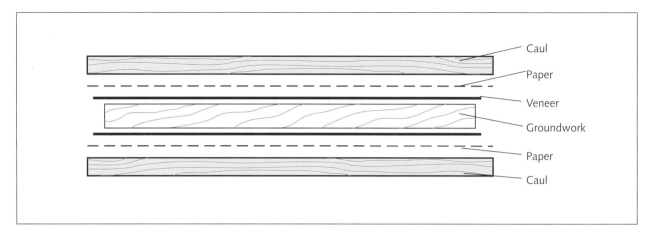

Fig 5.26 Positioning the various components in the press.

time. Even pearl glue can be used, provided a means of applying heat is employed (*see* page 19). If work is to be counter veneered, this should be done prior to laying the show and balance veneers, as a separate operation. Any joints required need to be prepared prior to laying.

USING THE CAULS

The purpose of the cauls is to apply even pressure over the whole surface until the glue has set. This pressure does not have to be enormous, as the purpose is simply to hold the veneer in continued contact with the adhesive on the ground. As the glue dries (or cures in the case of catalyzed adhesives, such as Cascamite) it will do the rest. However, it is important that the veneer is placed carefully on the ground and that any air pockets are expelled by rolling the veneer down first, using a photographic roller or decorators' seam roller. (Photographic rollers can be bought from a photographic equipment shop and a decorators' wallpaper seam roller can be bought from most DIY stores that stock decorating materials.) The veneer should be rolled down to remove trapped air and excess glue, making a good contact with the glued groundwork. Roll the veneer from the centre out towards the edges, but do not stretch it.

The glues most commonly used are those that are 'cold setting', i.e. they do not require heat to make them set or bond. Pearl glue can be used for restoration work for example, but a source of heat is needed in the form of heated, non-ferrous metal sheets.

Fig 5.27 Tightening the bolts on the bearers to generate pressure.

Figures 5.26 to 5.28 illustrate how the various components are packed between the cauls, assuming a cold setting glue is used. For the sake of simplicity, counter veneers have been excluded from the illustration, though these would have been laid before the show and balance veneers. The purpose of the sheets of paper covering the balance and show veneers is to prevent the cauls from sticking to the work should any glue find its way onto the surface. Ideally, this should not arise unless too much has been put onto the ground or you have not been working very cleanly (and it is very easy to transfer glue from the ground to the veneer surface).

To apply pressure to the bearers, first tighten the middle bearer carefully, so that the curve along its

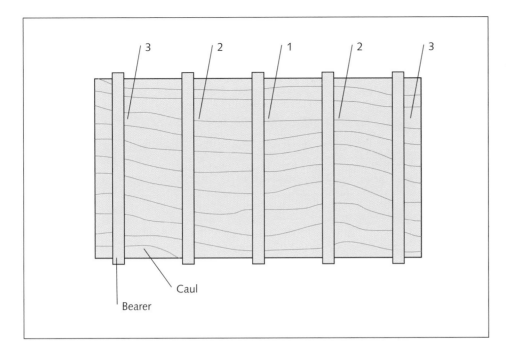

lower edge applies pressure gradually from the centre of the caul towards the edge. The whole process operates by applying pressure from the centre, working outwards along the length and width of the cauls. Surplus glue, if there is any, will be squeezed out rather than be trapped and cause a lump or crease in the veneer.

The work looks a mass of clamps and bearers when everything has been completed! For larger pieces it is useful to have a helper, working on the opposite side from you. This speeds up the process and also helps to ensure that pressure is applied evenly, as you synchronize the clamp tightening. The work should be kept under pressure overnight before being released and cleaned up (*see* page 72).

USING PEARL GLUE

Pearl glue cannot be used for the 'cold' pressing method described above, but it can be used with the caul press if some means of heating the glue is provided. This is usually in the form of a lightweight sheet of non-ferrous metal (ferrous metals will rust with the moisture, and may stain the work), heated until it is just about bearable to hold, and positioned between the sheet of paper and the caul, as shown in Fig 5.29. Remember, you will need two metal sheets if you are veneering both sides. It can be a cumbersome process and really does require a helper if the work is large. A heated metal sheet can also be used to shorten the setting time of cold setting glues (e.g. PVA,

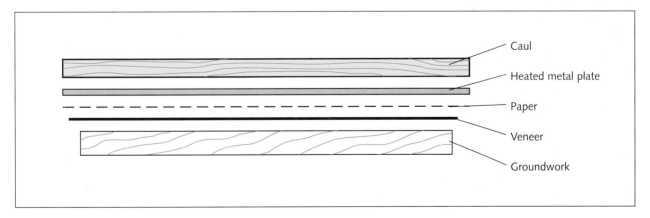

Fig 5.29 A heated, non-ferrous metal sheet is used to lay veneers with pearl glue.

Cascamite), thereby reducing the time needed to keep the work in the press.

The use of heat is an added complication, and there is a limited need for it now that we have reliable cold setting adhesives. However, authentic restoration work will require this method of laying veneers, especially for complex built-up patterns (such as marquetry or parquetry) that cannot be laid using the hammer method. Where joints are required in the work, these must be prepared prior to laying.

Some means of heating the metal sheets needs to be devised (e.g. using a hot air gun or an oven set on a low temperature if the metal is small enough) and the temperature should not be so high as to scorch the veneer or generate steam! Speed is required to prevent the sheets cooling down before they are placed on the work – hence the helper. Paradoxically, pearl glue gives you more time for positioning as it can be applied to the ground and allowed to chill and gel, at which point there is no great urgency. The same cannot be said of PVA, which will begin to set fairly soon after application (depending upon ambient air temperature). Therefore, plan the work so that the ground is glued, the veneer placed in position and covered with a single layer of paper (to prevent the metal sticking to the veneer), and the metal sheet laid over this as quickly as possible. Finally, position the wooden cauls and bearers, and apply the clamps.

MAKING A SIMPLE JOINT

1 Mark the position of the joint on the groundwork.

2 Cut the veneers slightly oversize so that they overhang the edges of the groundwork. This will allow for trimming after laying.

3 Cut the joining edge on each sheet of veneer, using a straightedge and a knife. The edges may look close when you put them together, but for high quality work, they should be planed on the shooting board as well, to get them perfectly true. (*See* Fig 3.11.) The two veneers should be placed one on the other and planed together to ensure that both edges are identical.

4 Place the veneers side by side, holding the joining edges in close contact, and tape the joint together, both across the joint, to hold the edges together, and along it. Take care not to pull too hard on the tape, as this will cause the veneers to buckle. There is no need to keep the joint under tension – it is sufficient to simply hold it together closely.

5 Draw heavy lines on the groundwork, corresponding to the position of any veneer joints, and use these as markers when placing the veneer on the ground prior to laying. Even with glue on the groundwork, these lines will be visible. Occasionally, the veneer will slip a fraction as pressure is applied on the bearers so, if exact positioning of the veneer is vital, you should drive several veneer pins into the work, and pinch these off at the surface so that they do not stand proud. When the work is removed from the caul press, use a very small nail punch to push the pins below the surface and a little stopping to fill the very small holes.

6 Clean and trim the veneer (*see* page 72).

SCREW PRESS

A screw press allows both surfaces of the ground to be veneered at the same time, and has the ability to create very high pressure. Whatever form of press is used, pressure need only be applied for the duration of the glue's setting time. In industrial terms, this time is a problem as the machine is tied up until the glue has set. Clearly, the longer this takes, the less productive the press will be. For this reason, companies whose main business is preparing veneered panels use heated presses that set the glue in a fraction of the time it takes to set at room temperature, and use resin glues specially formulated to cure quickly with heat. A small screw press is a useful addition to the home workshop, but commercial shops are called upon to produce veneered work on a regular basis so, for them, a larger press is indispensable. The principle for both is the same, except that the pressure plates in the commercial press are in sections, which allows the pressure to be applied in the centre first, then at the ends.

Veneers are prepared for the screw press as for the caul press, with pre-jointing of sheets and lines drawn on the groundwork corresponding to the position of any veneer joints.

Balance and show veneers are laid at the same time, with paper placed between the plates of the press and the veneer to prevent sticking.

It is a common belief that there is a need to apply very great pressure to ensure bonding of the veneer to the groundwork. This is not so. In fact, excessive pressure may cause difficulties if too much glue has been used, as lumps will form where the excess glue has been unable to escape. The general rule of thumb is to use a very thin layer of glue on the groundwork and enough pressure simply to maintain close contact. The glue will do the rest. As in caul veneering, both sides of the groundwork can be veneered at the same time. If you are using a counter veneer, remember to lay it on both sides, as a single operation, before laying the balance and show veneers.

SAND BOX

This is a very old technique, now superseded by the vacuum press. Nonetheless, if the veneering of shaped work is not a routine and regular operation, this technique is very useful. As far as authentic restoration work is concerned, where the use of pearl glue is the essential part of the process, the sand box remains an important means of veneering shaped work that cannot be tackled with the veneer hammer.

Dry silver sand is packed into a 'box' or other large, open container (*see* Fig 5.30). The sand can be warmed in an oven – to about 193°F (75°C) – if pearl glue is used, or if you want to speed up the setting time of resin glue.

CROSS VENEERING WITH THE SAND BOX

Cross veneering, with the grain of the veneer running across the width of the groundwork rather than along its length, was popular during the reign of William and Mary, and so is a useful method for restoration work. The example illustrated in Figs 5.31 and 5.32, shows cross veneering.

1 Press the object to be veneered into the sand and hold it with cramps to make an impression of its profile in the sand (*see* Fig 5.31). It is important to form this contour in the sand before you attempt to lay the veneer, because the sand will act as a shaped caul.

2 Remove the piece from the sand and prepare it to receive the veneer (*see* pages 50–2).

3 Prepare the veneer and cut a little oversize to allow for trimming and cleaning up (*see* Chapter 4). Prepare any necessary joints.

4 Glue the groundwork. (If the sand has been heated for using pearl glue, it will retain heat for a

Fig 5.30 A sand box suitable for veneering the shaped groundwork.

Fig 5.31 The groundwork is pressed into the sand, under the pressure of cramps, to create a reverse profile. In effect, the sand will act as a shaped caul.

long time, so there is less urgency about the process, but it is still advisable to prepare the veneer first before gluing groundwork.)

5 Place the veneer carefully on the groundwork and hold it in place with veneer pins. If possible, use the veneer pins on areas that will form waste. *Alternatively*, moisten the veneer, press it into the sand profile with the groundwork cramped over it to hold it in position and help form the shape, and leave it to dry for a couple of hours. When you release the pressure, the veneer will have taken on the shape of the groundwork (see Fig 5.32). This 'pre-forming' of the veneer makes it easier to position the veneer on the ground for gluing.

6 Apply glue to the groundwork, carefully position the veneer on it, and press them into the sand contour, applying pressure with cramps.

7 Clean up and trim the veneer (*see* page 72).

VACUUM PRESS

While the sand box method is very useful for occasional use on small jobs, if shaped work is to be regularly veneered, a vacuum press is

indispensable. For this, a means of generating a vacuum is needed and this can be in the form of a vacuum pump, or the intake side of an air compressor (*see* Chapter 3). The ground and veneer are placed on a baseboard inside a strong envelope, which is then sealed, and from which the air is removed. The envelope collapses as the air is withdrawn and presses the veneer down on the ground. The method can be used for flat and

Fig 5.32 The veneer can be 'pre-formed' to take on the shape of the groundwork, making it easier to glue it onto the ground later.

shaped work – including compound shapes – as it does not require the use of a solid component for applying the pressure. The envelopes are available in a range of sizes (*see* Suppliers on page 156). Vacuum press kits are available and it is advisable to buy one of these rather than attempt to make up your own press because they are made specifically for the purpose of veneering, will have full instructions on how to set up and use the press safely, and will conform to current safety regulations.

LAYING VENEER WITH THE VACUUM PRESS

1 Prepare the ground and veneer (*see* pages 39–52).

2 If not already present, rout grooves along the surface of the baseboard. This allows for even extraction of the air. As air is extracted from the vacuum press, the envelope will collapse, and the grooves running along the baseboard make it easier for the air to be drawn out.

3 Place the ground on the board, with the surface to be veneered facing upwards, and place flaring pieces on either end to even out the pull on the bag as the air is extracted (*see* Fig 5.33).

4 Glue the ground, place the veneer carefully over it, and secure its position with veneer pins, pinched off at the surface.

5 Cover the work with paper to prevent the bag from sticking to it, and place the whole arrangement of baseboard, groundwork and veneer into the bag.

6 Seal one end of the bag, which is open-ended like a tube, by clamping a strip of wood across it.

7 Seal the other end of the tube around the air extraction tube, which is attached to the vacuum pump, and place a thumbscrew, or whatever device is supplied with the press, over the extraction tube.

8 Start the vacuum pump, and adjust the bag to prevent it creasing as the air is extracted. The bag's surface *must* lie flat against the work, as creases will cause a local loss of pressure. There is also the possibility that the bag will work its way under the edge of the veneer if it is not kept flat and straight.

9 When the air has been extracted, switch off the pump, and close off the tube with the thumbscrew, to maintain the vacuum.

10 Leave the press like this until the glue has set so that it maintains a constant pressure on the work. To remove the work from the press, slowly release the closure on the extraction tube to allow the air back in – the grooves in the baseboard will help with this as well – and relax the bag. Once the vacuum has been completely eliminated by the entry of air, the bag can be opened and the work removed for cleaning up and finishing (*see* Cleaning Up, page 72).

Fig 5.33 Placing the groundwork and veneer on the baseboard, ready for the envelope. Note the flaring pieces at the edges of the work.

TABLE 5.1: COMPARATIVE TABLE OF VENEER LAYING METHODS

METHOD	CHARACTERISTICS
GLUE FILM AND CONTACT ADHESIVES	Require no complex or expensive veneer pressing equipment. Suitable for laying single sheets of veneer on a flat surface, or on simple shaped work, such as the frieze of a round table top. Not suitable for laying veneers on more complicated shapes with tight curves, or for laying veneers that require jointing (the veneer can be stretched and the joint opened during laying).
HAMMER VENEERING	Requires no complex or expensive veneer pressing equipment. Requires the use of pearl glue. Can be used for work that requires veneers to be jointed and for simple shaped work. There are better methods for laying more complex built-up patterns, such as quartering, but the hammer method can be used. Hammer veneering is an appropriate method for restoration work.
CAUL PRESS	A relatively inexpensive form of veneer press, ideal when using cold setting glues such as PVA or Cascamite. Only suitable for flat work, and any built-up patterns, such as quartering and cross-banding, must be jointed prior to laying. The size of the work that can be veneered by this method is limited only by the size of the cauls that can be made and the availability of suitable clamps! An ideal method for the occasional craftsman or for the small workshop where large equipment would be a problem. The method can be used for all veneering techniques, including marquetry and parquetry. In restoration work that uses pearl glue, heated cauls can be used.
SCREW PRESS	A relatively expensive and bulky piece of equipment. Small presses are ideal for marquetry work. Only suitable for flat work and normally with cold setting glues. It is possible to use intervening hot metal plates for use with animal glue (as in caul veneering). Larger veneered work will require expensive equipment that is really only suitable for commercial workshops.
SAND BOX	An inexpensive way of veneering shaped work with cold setting or animal glues. The size of the work is limited only by the size of the box you can make. Generally though, the method is used for relatively small work, such as curved cupboard doors, or veneered cornices and other mouldings. Jointing of veneers is necessary before laying (e.g. cross-banding, parquetry). If the sand is heated, pearl glue can be used, making it ideal for restoring shaped work.
VACUUM PRESS	In a sense, this is the ultimate veneer press. It is expensive, but can be used on any type of work – flat, shaped, marquetry, parquetry. Industrial vacuum presses are also able to apply heat to cure the glue more rapidly. Presses suitable for the small workshop are only suitable for cold setting glues. The equipment for small workshops is portable and can be stored away easily, taking up very little space when not in use. A worthwhile investment for anyone undertaking regular veneering work – and it does away with the need for large numbers of clamps and bearers!

REQUIREMENTS (in addition to groundwork and veneers)	
For glue film	**For contact adhesive**
● Glue film and its backing paper ● Clothes iron ● Veneer hammer or a roller	● Contact adhesive (e.g. Evo-Stik) ● Brown wrapping paper (i.e. the type with a shiny surface) ● Veneer hammer or a roller
● Pearl glue prepared in a double boiler or glue pot, and glue brush ● Clothes iron ● Veneer hammer	● Veneer tape (for joints) ● Brown wrapping paper ● Veneer knife and straightedge to make joints when required
● Cauls and bearers ● One pair of cramps or heavy-duty bolts per pair of bearers ● Cold setting glue (e.g. Evo-Stik Resin W or other PVA, Cascamite) ● Veneer knife and straightedge to make joints if required ● Veneer tape to secure joints	● Veneer pins ● Template to build up the veneers to a pattern where required ● Plain paper to prevent cauls sticking to the work during pressing ● Warmed zinc plates (heated cauls) to accelerate glue setting if desired
● Screw press ● Cold setting glue (e.g. Evo-Stik Resin W or other PVA, Cascamite) ● Veneer knife and straightedge to make joints if required ● Veneer tape to secure joints ● Veneer pins	● Template to build up the veneers to a pattern where required ● Plain paper to prevent cauls sticking to the work during pressing ● Warmed zinc plates (heated cauls) to accelerate glue setting if desired
● Silver sand and a retaining box (wooden is best) ● Cold setting or animal glue are suitable ● Veneer knife and straightedge to make joints ● Clamps to maintain pressure on the groundwork during pressing	● Veneer pins to secure veneers ● Veneer tape to secure any joints
● Commercially available vacuum press kit ● Cold setting glue ● Veneer knife and straightedge to make joints if required	● Veneer pins to secure work ● Veneer tape to secure joints ● Template for building up the design

CLEANING UP

Further work on the veneered object to prepare it for final finishing and polishing can only take place after it has been removed from the press: in the press, there is no possibility of access. However, there are two exceptions to this – when the work has been hammer veneered or when it has been ironed down with glue film.

Glue film has the advantage of being 'clean', i.e. glue does not find its way onto the upper surface of the veneer. Also, there is little, if any, surplus glue oozing from the edges so cleaning up is easy. If you leave the veneered work for half an hour or so, the glue will have hardened sufficiently to allow excess veneer to be safely trimmed away as described below. When hammer veneering, the work must be left for several hours at least before attempting to trim excess veneer from around the edge. The edges of veneered work are always vulnerable while the glue is drying and hardening. Attempting to trim the edges before the glue has had time to set may result in the edge lifting.

When the work comes out of the press, it will require cleaning up to remove any veneer tape and excess glue, and the excess veneer also needs to be removed.

To remove tape, moisten it with warm water to soften it, and peel off as much as possible. Any remaining stubborn pieces can then be removed with a blunt scraper. It should be worked along the length of the tape that is being removed. The grain direction of the veneer is not an important consideration, and the scraper can be worked in any direction because its purpose is to remove surface debris rather than smooth the veneer itself. However, do take care if a veneer joint is a little lumpy, which sometimes happens, so as not to tear out the lump altogether. If this does happen, you will need to treat it as a blemish and fill it with wood filler, if very minor, or patch it if the damage cannot be easily masked with filler. (*See* Patching a Hole, page 44.)

Overlapping veneer at the edges can be removed in a number of ways, depending on the size and shape of the object.

For small pieces, it can simply be cut off with a craft knife, and the edge gently sanded smooth. For large pieces, however, this is a laborious task, and

Fig 5.34 A self-guided laminate trimmer and router is ideal for quick and accurate removal of the excess veneer.

the pieces can be difficult to handle. For these, the router is invaluable, especially for long or shaped edges.

With square and rectangular work an ordinary straight cutter is fine, when used with its fence, but where sides are not straight, a special laminate trimming cutter is required. These cutters are self-guided, in that they have a small wheel, or guide, which rests against the edge of the groundwork, preventing the cutter from straying into the body of the work (*see* Fig 5.34). The wheel should be held tight against the work so that the cutter trims back the excess veneer while following its perimeter. The edge can then be gently sanded to remove any roughness.

If you are trimming by hand, with a knife, trim away any pieces that need to be cut across the grain before edges where the grain is lengthways. This reduces the risk of splitting out the veneer in much the same way as when you are cutting the veneer to size prior to laying (*see* page 40).

Once the surface has been cleaned and the excess veneer trimmed and smoothed, the work is ready for sanding smooth, staining and finishing as required (*see* Chapter 11).

REPAIRING BLISTERS AND LIFTED EDGES

Occasionally, the veneer may not be properly bonded to the ground, and this leads to blisters and lifting edges. Unfortunately, because we are unable to see what is happening inside the press, preventive or remedial action cannot be taken before the glue has had time to set: repairs must be undertaken after the event, when it is the most difficult time to do so.

BLISTERS

These may be caused by a localized lack of glue or pressure. The approach to repairing them depends on the type of glue used. In the case of pearl glue, localized heat can be used to liquefy the glue, and then pressure can be applied to the area, with a small wooden block cramped onto the surface, until the glue sets (*see* Fig 5.35). Place a sheet of paper over the veneer to prevent it from sticking to the veneered surface should any glue seep out.

In the case of cold-setting glues, such as PVA or Cascamite, the blister must be split by cutting along the grain with a veneer knife, so that fresh glue can be inserted underneath, and pressure applied to the area until the new glue sets (*see* Figs 5.36 and 5.37). Here again, paper is placed over the veneer to prevent the weight sticking to it.

If you are careful and cut directly along the grain without damaging the surface, the blister will

Fig 5.36 **Splitting a blister along the grain and inserting fresh glue with an artists' palette knife.**

usually glue down without difficulty. Sometimes, the two edges of the cut don't meet, or may overlap a little. Any slight gap can be filled with a proprietary wood filler. An overlap may be a little more difficult to deal with in that you may need to sand it flat – since it won't be a large lump. If this creates a small gap, it can also be filled prior to staining and polishing.

LIFTED EDGES

These are treated in the same way as blisters except that as there is access to the ground, it is unnecessary to cut the veneer. Glue can be slipped under the edge using a fine artists' palette knife before applying localized pressure until the glue sets.

Fig 5.35 **Pressing down blisters. Note the paper which prevents the wooden block sticking to the veneer.**

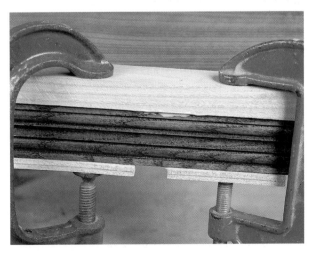

Fig 5.37 **Cramping the edge after the glue has been slipped under it.**

6

CROSS-BANDING

- ◆ PREPARATION

- ◆ LAYING CROSS-BANDING WITH VENEER
  HAMMER AND PEARL GLUE

- ◆ LAYING CROSS-BANDING WITH A PRESS

- ◆ SIMPLE BUILT-UP PATTERNS

PREPARATION

There are many ways of providing additional decoration to a veneered surface: cross-banding is the most straightforward of these. Its effect is to frame a central panel of veneer and it is at its most striking when the cross-banding veneer is of a contrasting colour or species. It is also quite common to insert an intervening inlay string or banding between the main panel and the cross-banding. (*See* Chapter 8.)

Historically, another function of cross-banding was to act as a protection for the panel itself. Pearl glue in the early days was less reliable, and it was easier to repair a damaged cross-banding than a highly decorative and valuable veneer. Modern glues, however, are very powerful adhesives, so the protective function is far less important.

As with simple veneers, you must remember to use counter veneers and/or balancing veneers with built-up patterns, but it is not necessary to add cross-banding to these.

Cross-banding veneers are prepared from a piece of straight-grained veneer. It is usual for the grain direction to be at right angles to the edge of the

central veneer panel (*see* Fig 6.1), but sometimes work has the grain running parallel to the panel edge (*see* Fig 6.2). Using a straightedge and veneer knife, cut strips of the veneer ³⁄₈in (10mm) wider than the eventual width of the cross-banding, making sure they are all the same width. This ensures an overlap at the edge of the groundwork to allow for trimming after the glue has dried. The internal edge that butts up against the central panel should be trued up on the shooting board with a very sharp and finely set plane.

It will often be necessary to join strips of the cross-band to make up the required length (*see* page 44) so cut and true up the edges of enough strips to go all round the work.

How the central panel of veneer is prepared depends on how the veneers will be laid. Hammer veneering and press veneering each require a different approach. In the case of hammer veneering, the central panel is laid first, trimmed to size, and then the cross-bands are added. If the veneers are to be pressed, the cross-band and central panel are usually prepared and pre-jointed so that the whole assembled pattern is laid in one operation.

Fig 6.1 Cross-banding usually has the grain direction at right angles to the edge of the central veneer panel.

Fig 6.2 Another option is to lay the border with its grain direction running parallel to the edge of the work.

LAYING CROSS-BANDING WITH VENEER HAMMER AND PEARL GLUE

SQUARE OR RECTANGULAR WORK

When laying cross-banding, it may be necessary to use two or more pieces adjacent to each other. The following general method assumes that this is the case, with some modifications given for variations in design.

1 Prepare the central panel of veneer so that its overall size is smaller than the groundwork. The border for the cross-banding is prepared by cutting back the central panel to a fixed distance from the edge using a cutting gauge. Since the gauge has a fence that needs to be held tight against the edge of the groundwork, any excess veneer that overhangs the edge will prevent the use of the gauge.

2 Brush pearl glue over the groundwork in which the central panel will be laid, and allow the glue to gel.

3 Lay the veneer with the clothes iron and veneer hammer.

4 Trim the excess veneer from the central panel with a cutting gauge set at a distance equal to the width of the cross-banding. With the fence hard against the edge of the groundwork, trim the excess veneer. This ensures that the edge of the panel is parallel with the side of the groundwork (*see* Fig 6.3). It is essential that the veneer is cut through completely in one pass if an even edge is to be made.

5 Use a chisel to lift off the waste veneer.

6 Before laying, brush a thin layer of glue over the back of the cross-banding and allow to gel. This will compensate for the glue that is removed when the veneer panel is trimmed. You should expect the

Fig 6.3 The central panel
of veneer stands some
way in from the edge.

veneer to curl with the heat and moisture – this is
not a problem.

7 Lay the cross-banding around the edge, making
a close joint with the central panel and laying each
piece separately. Slightly moisten the upper surface
of the cross-banding (to help counteract the curling
that has taken place), position along one side of
the work, butting against the central panel, and
iron it down. As the glue melts, the veneer will
tend to float, so take care that it maintains a close
joint. Tape the joint between the cross-banding and
the panel.

If more than one piece is needed to cover the
length of a side, take a second piece of cross-
banding and repeat the process, but ensure that it
overlaps the first piece. Make a joint in the overlap
by laying a straightedge over it and cutting through
both veneers in one pass, working from the outside
edge towards the central panel. Tape the joint, and
continue with this process until all the cross-
banding has been laid.

8 Make up the corners. For square corners, butt
or mitre joints can be used (*see* Fig 6.4). Mitred
corners provide a picture frame effect, while butt

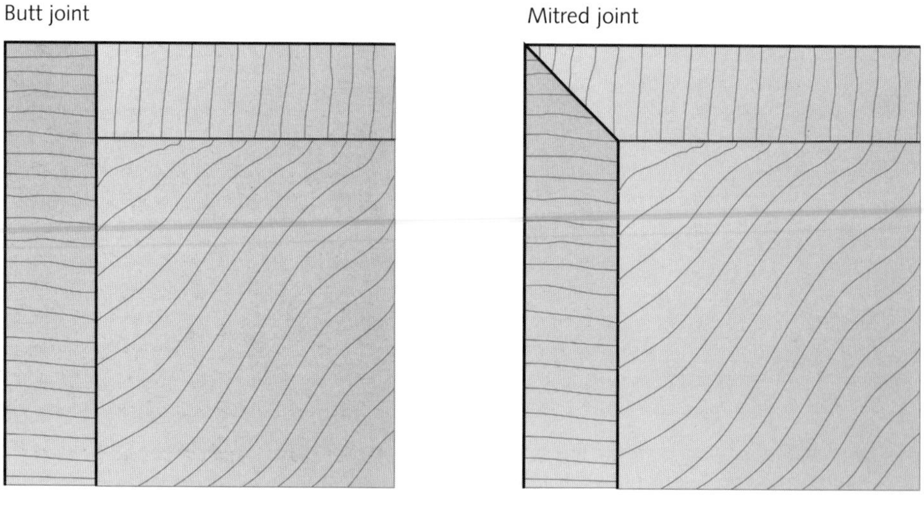

Butt joint

Mitred joint

Fig 6.4 The two main
types of joint.

joints give the look of a frame and panel construction.

To make a butt joint, you must first decide which lengths of cross-banding will continue through from end to end. These are usually those on the longest sides of the work, with the short sides butting up against them. Lay these two short sides first, making the length slightly longer than that of the central panel (*see* Fig 6.5). With a

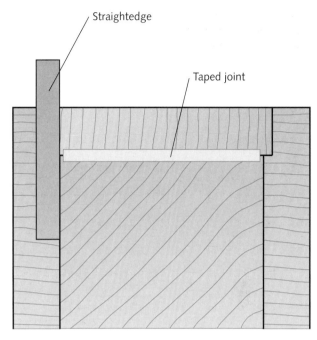

Fig 6.6 To trim the cross-banding to length, hold the straightedge against the long edge of the central panel.

straightedge and veneer knife, trim the ends of the cross-banding so that the length of the cross-banding is equal to the width of the panel (*see* Fig 6.6). Lay both short, butting cross-bands before adding the longer ones. Tape the joints between the cross-band and the central panel as each is completed. Lay the other two sides, again taping the joints as you go (*see* Fig 6.7).

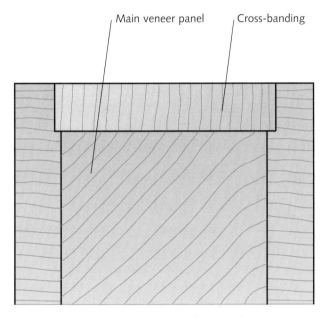

Fig 6.5 In making butt joints, the shorter sides are laid first, slightly longer than the edge of the veneer panel to allow for trimming.

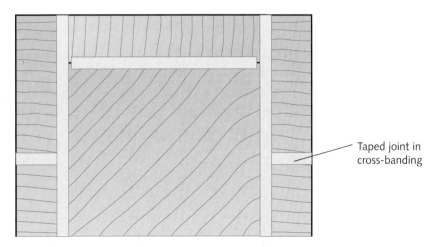

Fig 6.7 The long sides of cross-banding are laid and the joints taped.

For a mitred joint, adjacent sides should be cross-banded and left with the veneer overlapping at the corner (*see* Fig 6.8). To make the mitre, use a straightedge and veneer knife to cut diagonally through both veneers at the corner, ensuring that the join passes over the corner of the ground. If the cross-banding has been cut to the same width all round, as should be done, then a diagonal cut through the corner of the overlap will make a 45° mitre. Remove the waste pieces, run the iron over the cross-banding to re-melt the glue, and rub down with the veneer hammer. Tape the joint.

A If larger pieces are used, the resulting grain direction will make the mismatch obvious

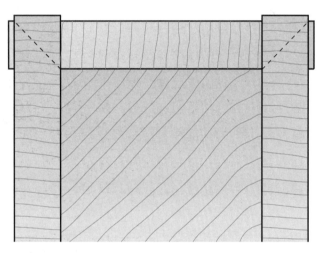

Fig 6.8 To make a mitred joint, overlap the cross-banding at the corners.

B To maintain the direction of the grain at right angles to the central panel at rounded corners, the cross-banding needs to be laid as small sections

Fig 6.9 Laying cross-banding on a rounded corner.

A slight complication is presented by rounded corners, for which neither of the above methods is appropriate. The effect of cross-banding relies on the grain direction being at 90° to the edge of the central panel and using large pieces at the corner will show a mismatch of grain direction (*see* Fig 6.9A). To avoid this, cross-banding for a rounded corner is made up from a number of smaller sections rather than from a single, or a couple, of larger pieces (*see* Fig 6.9B).

To make a rounded corner, cut round a template (*see* Fig 6.10), and then use the same template for preparing the cross-band at the corner, which needs

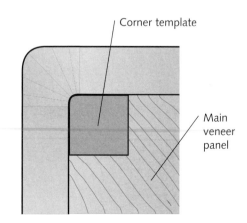

Fig 6.10 Use a template to trim the corner of the central panel and remove the waste veneer.

Fig 6.11 Prefabricate the veneer for the corner: it is a lot easier than trying to lay several small sections of veneer with accurate joints.

veneer directly into place (*see* Fig 6.13) by sliding it into position. Secure it by applying a little pressure with the veneer hammer – too much may dislodge the veneer. Position all the corners in this way and then fit the rest of the cross-banding up to them, making whatever joints are necessary as described above.

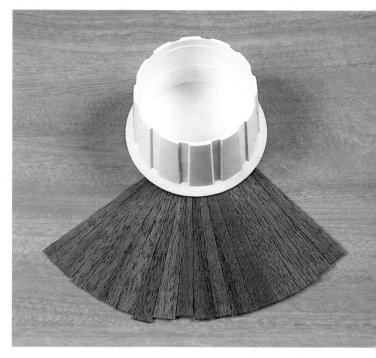

to be made up before laying (*see* Fig 6.11). Cut small wedges of veneer to fit the template, and butt them together, taping the joints securely. Prepare all the corners in advance, using the template to make the inner curved edge (*see* Fig 6.12).

The easiest way to lay a prefabricated corner is by 'rubbing' it onto the edge. To do this, brush a thin layer of glue onto the veneer's undersurface and, while it is still hot and fluid, press the corner

Fig 6.12 Use the template to make the inner curved edge to the corner cross-banding.

Fig 6.13 'Rubbing' the prefabricated corner into place. This is done by sliding the veneer into position. The natural 'grab' of pearl glue will hold it in place.

ROUNDED OR CURVED WORK

Straight-edged work presents few complications, but as soon as a curvature is introduced, there is the difficulty of ensuring a close-fitting joint between the cross-banding and the central panel, whose edge generally follows the shape of the groundwork. Inevitably, the cross-banding will need to be fitted as a series of short pieces.

1 Prepare and lay the central panel as you would for square work.

2 Trim the panel with the cutting gauge, which needs to be modified for curved work. The normal fence is designed for straight edges. When used on a curved edge it will rock, making it impossible to get a good edge to the central panel. To prevent this rocking, and to keep the blade working at the same distance all round, glue two dowels to the fence, as shown in Fig 6.14.

3 Add the cross-banding in short pieces so that the curve of the groundwork can be negotiated, and at the same time, ensure that the grain direction is generally at right angles to the centre, and there is no obvious mismatch. The length of individual pieces depends on the degree of curvature, so you need to take each situation as it comes.

4 No matter how long you make each piece, the straight edge of the cross-banding will not make a perfect joint with the central veneer. To make a good joint, hollow the edge of the cross-banding slightly. This is easier on deeper curves, and this should be taken into consideration when deciding how long to make each piece of cross-banding. Making a template of the curve will make life easier when preparing each piece, though in work where there are curves of different radii (e.g. a kidney-shaped dressing table), preparation needs to be free hand. Experience will enable you to judge how accurate you can be, but as a rule of thumb, the shorter the veneer, the more accurate you are likely to be.

5 Brush a thin layer of pearl glue on the veneer and 'rub' it into place. The natural property of the glue to grab will keep it in place without the need to apply pressure.

6 Position the remaining pieces of cross-banding, making the joints between them as described above. Tape all the joints, both between pieces of cross-banding and between the cross-banding and the central veneer panel.

Fig 6.14 A modified cutting gauge for working with curved groundwork.

LAYING CROSS-BANDING WITH A PRESS

SQUARE OR RECTANGULAR WORK

1 Cut the central veneer panel to shape and size, and trim. To ensure that the edges are all true and square, this should be done on the shooting board.

2 Mark the layout of the veneer pattern on the groundwork to show the positioning of the central panel and the cross-banding (*see* Fig 6.15). This aids accurate positioning of the veneer for laying.

3 Mark out a piece of thin ply in the same way, and use this as a baseboard to assemble the veneers, before positioning them on the groundwork (*see* Fig 6.16). While the use of a baseboard as a template is essential for the more complex veneer patterns, it is not necessary for simple, built-up patterns. All the same, it is convenient to work on a template rather than on the groundwork itself.

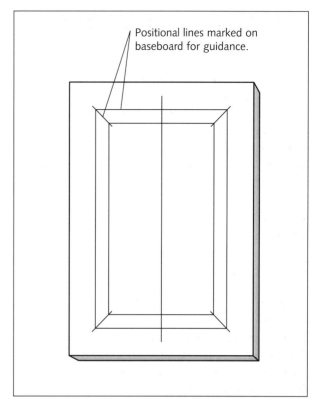

Positional lines marked on baseboard for guidance.

Fig 6.16 The use of a baseboard marked out as a template is very useful for assembling the various components. For more complex patterns, a template is essential.

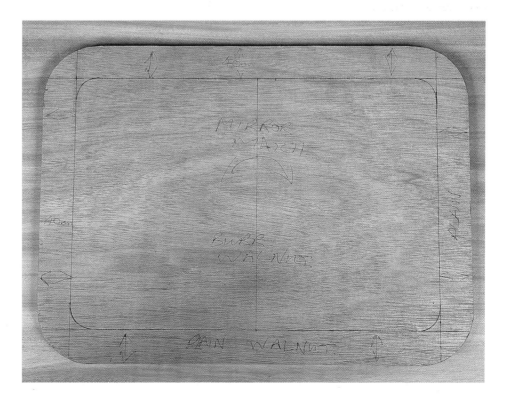

Fig 6.15 For press work, mark out the groundwork to show the positions of the central panel and cross-banding.

Fig 6.17 The central panel is held in place with veneer pins while fitting the cross-banding.

Fig 6.18 The cross-banding fitted and taped to the central panel. The overlap at the corners is suitable for a butt joint.

overlap is particularly important for mitred corners, as adjacent pieces of cross-band are joined by cutting through the overlap with a straightedge and knife (*see* page 78). The cut should be at right angles to the edge of the panel. Mitred, butt and rounded corners are all created as for hammer veneering.

8 Lay and press the veneer.

ROUND, OVAL AND SHAPED WORK

1 Make a template of the central panel. Acrylic plastic sheet is ideal for this because it can be cut and shaped with woodcutting saws. Smooth the perimeter of the template with abrasive paper, so that the veneer knife will work around the edge to cut the veneer without snagging on any roughness. You should also place some registration or alignment marks on the top of the template to assist with lining up the veneer on the ground. Figure 6.19 shows the geometry of oval- and kidney-shaped templates with the registration marks that can be used to help alignment.

2 Mark the groundwork with the same registration lines as the template. Position the template and draw around it to mark the position of the panel on the groundwork.

4 Position the central panel on the template, and hold it in place with veneer pins (*see* Fig 6.17). The veneer must be absolutely flat. If there is any sign of buckling, flatten the veneer (*see* Chapter 2, page 47).

5 Offer up a piece of the cross-band to the edge of the panel, ensure a close joint, and tape it securely into position.

6 Offer up a second piece so that it overlaps the end of the first piece by about $^3/_8$in (10mm) or so. Continue this process on all sides.

7 Fix the corners, remembering that they should overlap (*see* page 78, and Fig 6.18). A generous

Fig 6.19 The geometry of oval and kidney shapes: making the shaped templates, and to mark out the groundwork and assembly baseboard.

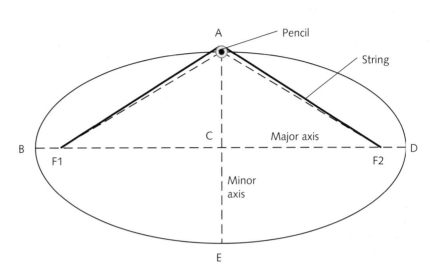

The perimeter of the ellipse is drawn with a pencil which is restrained by the string. The two ends of the string are held at the points F1 and F2 and the string is kept taut by the pencil as it scribes the perimeter. The lengths A–F1 and A–F2 are equal to the distance B–C. Therefore, to locate and mark the positions of the foci of the ellipse (i.e. F1 and F2), you use the distance B–C. The overall shape of the ellipse is determined by the dimensions you use for the major and minor axes.

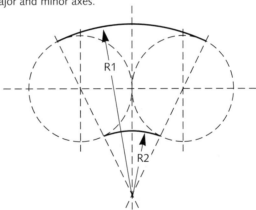

R1 and R2 are the radii of the arcs that form the links between the two circles forming the basis of the kidney shape.

3 Prepare the veneer panel by placing the template over the veneer, and cutting around it with a veneer knife. Take great care not to wander. This can happen very easily as the knife cuts along the grain.

4 Position the veneer on the groundwork, or a marked out baseboard, within the marked area, and secure it with veneer pins.

5 Offer up pieces of cross-banding to the edge of the panel, ensuring a close fit. Make the pieces relatively small, and shape their inner edges to make a close fit with the panel's curvature.

6 Cut and tape the joints between adjacent sections as well as between the cross-banding and central panel.

7 Lay and press the veneer.

LAYING THE VENEER

The principle of laying built-up veneers is the same as that for single sheets (*see* Chapter 5), except that the veneer must be accurately positioned on the ground. This is where marking out the groundwork pays dividends. Apply an even layer of glue to the ground and place the veneer so that the central panel lines up with the area marked. Cross-banding should overhang the groundwork a little to allow for trimming. Pay particular attention to mitred corners as these must be in line with the corners of the groundwork.

The veneers may become displaced slightly as pressure is applied in the press. To avoid this, put in a couple of veneer pins near the edge, pinching them off at the surface of the veneer. The difficulty with a press is that you cannot see any slippage happen, only its effect once you remove the work, at which point it is too late. Slippage is especially noticeable if the cross-banding is narrow, where it shows up as an obvious tapering towards the corners.

As always, a balancing veneer must be laid at the same time as the surface veneer.

ALTERNATIVE METHOD FOR LAYING

It is possible to carry out cross-banding in a two-stage pressing process. Superficially, the method resembles that used for laying with the hammer, but here the central panel is pressed onto the groundwork first. After removing the piece from the press, while the glue is still relatively soft, run a cutting gauge around the edge to trim back the central panel, and lift off the waste with a chisel. This method has a particular advantage when working with narrow cross-bandings and borders, as it ensures that the cross-banding will be parallel to the edge.

With PVA glue, you can usually remove the work from the press after about an hour, then trim and remove the waste veneer before the glue has completely dried, which makes the trimming process a good deal easier. Once this is done, the cross-banding can be fitted and the work returned to the press.

SIMPLE BUILT-UP PATTERNS

Figure 6.20 shows two examples of veneer designs based on a central panel of veneer surrounded by a cross-band or veneer border. They were both made with the use of a baseboard (which carries the design drawn on its surface, and upon which the veneers will be built-up prior to laying) and shaped templates to carry out accurate cutting of the veneer shapes themselves. It is a good deal easier to lay these designs in a press rather than by veneer hammer.

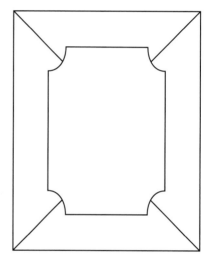

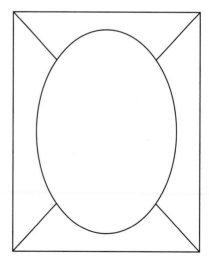

Fig 6.20 Examples of other built-up patterns.

BOOK-MATCHING AND QUARTERING

MATCHED PATTERNS

Highly decorative effects can be created without resorting to complicated techniques, simply by matching the patterns of adjacent veneers (*see* Fig 7.1). Part of the aesthetic quality of using veneers is to make the most of what the veneer has to offer with its colour and grain.

Because of the thinness of each leaf of veneer, consecutive leaves have more or less the same figure pattern, and it is this property on which veneering patterns rely. Even if the area to be covered is relatively small, where a single leaf would normally be enough for the job, you will still need consecutive leaves. This means that you may only use a small area of each leaf, so these methods do tend to be wasteful, and thus expensive. However, through careful choice of veneers, or areas of veneers, you may be able to save sections large enough to use in other projects.

The most important feature of highly decorative veneers, such as curls and burrs, is their uniqueness. No two pieces of veneer are exactly alike, but with highly decorative veneers, the difference is even greater. Even consecutive leaves will differ slightly, but usually not enough to be clearly noticeable.

While the most striking decorative effects are created by matching consecutive leaves of highly figured veneers such as curls and burrs, straight-grained veneers can also be used (*see* Fig 7.2). It is tempting to use just one sheet to create these effects, but that would be a mistake because the figure is not identical along the whole length of a leaf. This is hardly noticeable when viewing the whole sheet, but some very odd looking effects result if you start attempting to book-match or quarter (*see* Fig 7.3). The safest plan is to use consecutive leaves in all cases of mirror image or other veneer matching techniques. This is considerably more expensive, but as mentioned before, you can plan the work to reduce wastage and even to use the remaining sections in other pieces. In addition, one sheet can be cut to produce multiple panels. For example, by cutting two or four consecutive leaves down the middle, two book-matched or quartered panels, respectively, can be gained, giving the materials greater value for

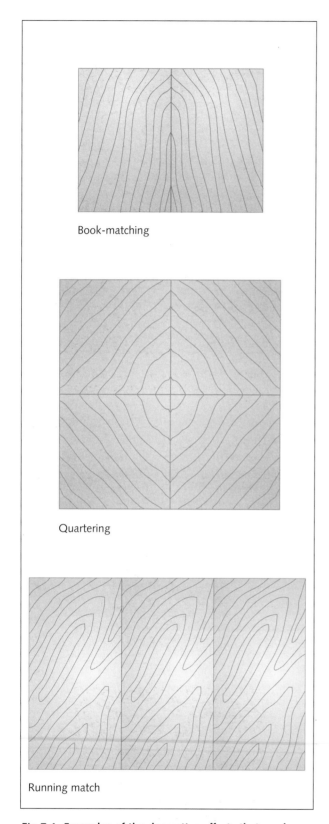

Book-matching

Quartering

Running match

Fig 7.1 Examples of the decorative effects that can be created very simply by matching grain and colour configuration.

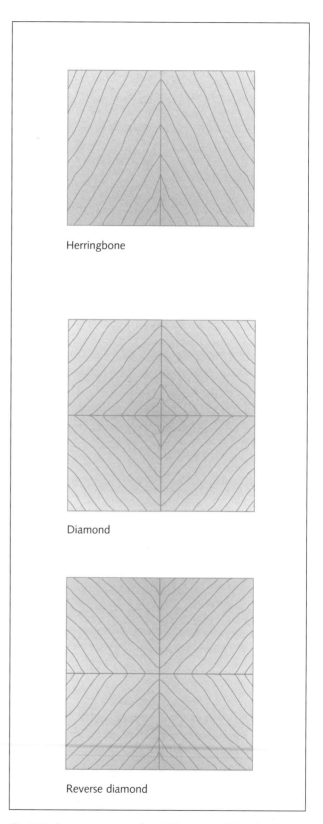

Herringbone

Diamond

Reverse diamond

Fig 7.2 Common ways of matching straight-grained veneers.

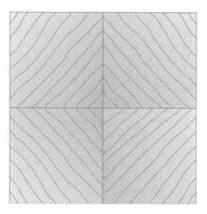

Fig 7.3 Optical defects that can result from not using consecutive leaves of straight-grained veneers.

money. An important point to remember when cutting packs of consecutive veneers is that you must keep the leaves in perfect alignment so that the figure of each leaf coincides.

MIRROR IMAGE

The decorative effects of book-matching and quartering are based on the mirror image principle (*see* Figs 7.4 and 7.5). In book-matching the mirror image is created by opening two consecutive leaves like the pages of a book, while for quartering, four consecutive leaves are used to create the mirror image twice (*see* Figs 7.6 and 7.7).

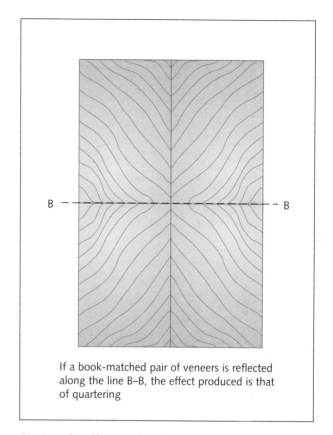

If a book-matched pair of veneers is reflected along the line B–B, the effect produced is that of quartering

Fig 7.5 The effect produced by quartering.

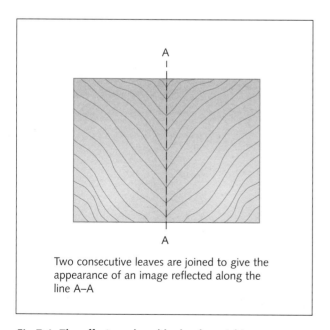

Two consecutive leaves are joined to give the appearance of an image reflected along the line A–A

Fig 7.4 The effect produced by book-matching.

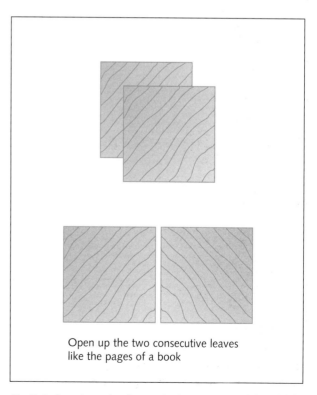

Open up the two consecutive leaves like the pages of a book

Fig 7.6 Creating a book-matched panel.

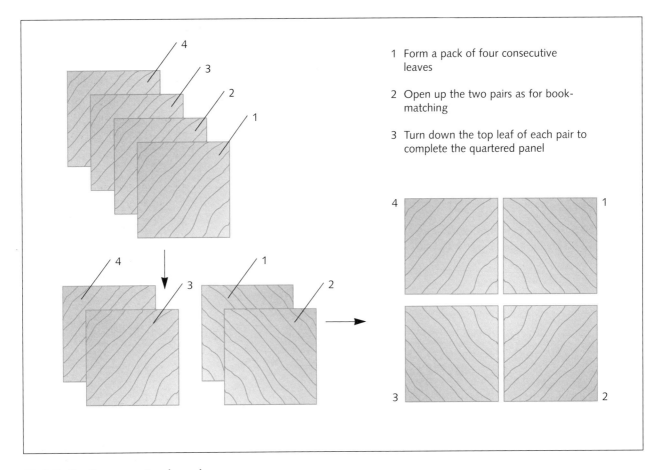

1 Form a pack of four consecutive leaves

2 Open up the two pairs as for book-matching

3 Turn down the top leaf of each pair to complete the quartered panel

Fig 7.7 Creating a quartered panel.

PREPARING THE VENEERS

While it is possible to lay book-matched or quartered veneers by hand – i.e. using pearl glue and the veneer hammer – there is the risk that they will not match at the joints, because of the need to cut through the overlap, which almost always results in a slight mismatch. For this reason, it is best to lay book-matched or quartered panels with a press of some description.

LAYING BOOK-MATCHED PANELS

1 Carefully position two consecutive leaves of veneer on top of each other, so that they are oriented in the way they came off the veneer cutting machine. Keep their edges closely aligned to ensure that the figuring of the two leaves coincides.

2 Choose the area of figure that you wish to use, planning your work carefully, and cut the pack to size, leaving a slight overlap to allow for final trimming. A veneer knife or saw can be used for this, with a straightedge, though the saw is often better for this trimming work, especially with hard or highly figured woods. You may find it helpful to tape the pack at the edges, to keep the veneers in place.

Remember when you are planning the cuts, that after opening up the leaves, the final size will be double the width of the pack. Be particularly careful when cutting along the side that will form the joint between the two veneers, as any splintering will require trimming, which may result in a noticeable mismatch.

3 Trim the joining edges of the two veneers very finely, on the shooting board: the edge produced by the knife or saw is unlikely to be good enough, especially with long joints. Do not overtrim, just skim the joint, because the more you remove, the greater the mismatch of figure after joining.

Leave the tape on, to help hold the veneers together, and use a batten of wood to hold the edges of the veneer flat and steady (*see* Fig 7.8).

4 Open out the top veneer, as though turning the pages of a book, to form the mirror image (*see* Fig 7.6), then fit and tape the joint. Take great care that the figure of both veneers lines up exactly at the joint, or it will look very odd.

5 Lay the veneer carefully and accurately.

Fig 7.8 Trim the joining edges on the shooting board. Note the use of a batten to hold the edges flat and secure.

LAYING QUARTERED PANELS

1 Carefully position four consecutive leaves of veneer on top of each other, orienting them in the way they came off the cutting machine, and keeping their edges closely aligned to ensure that their figuring coincides.

2 Choose the area of figure you wish to use: you need to visualize the completed pattern because the veneers must be positioned in a particular way in the pack in order to achieve that pattern (*see* Fig 7.9).

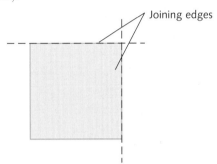

Fig 7.9 The orientation of the veneers in the trimmed pack determines the final pattern of the quartered panel. The dotted lines represent the sides that will make the joints between the component leaves in the panel.

3 Cut the panels to size as for book-matched panels (*see* page 88). This preparation of the veneers requires great care, as there will be two joining edges on each piece, and they must be at right angles to each other, though the initial cutting of the quarters can be approximate to within a few degrees.

Hold the veneers firmly in place with tape as you cut. The four layers take some cutting through, so it is better to use a veneer saw for this to ensure a neat job.

4 True up the joining edges, on the shooting board (*see* Fig 7.9). Keep the tape on and use a batten to hold down the veneer, to ensure that the pieces do not slip (*see* Fig 7.8). The fence of the shooting board is at 90° to the edge of the board, so to ensure that both edges are at right angles to each other, trim one jointing edge and then hold that edge firmly against the fence while you trim

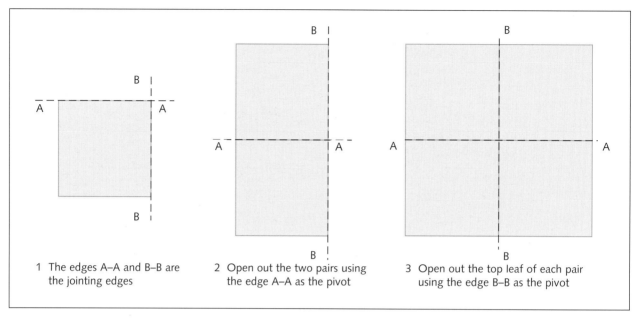

1 The edges A–A and B–B are the jointing edges

2 Open out the two pairs using the edge A–A as the pivot

3 Open out the top leaf of each pair using the edge B–B as the pivot

Fig 7.10 Opening out a quartered panel from a trimmed pack.

the other. This is vital if all the edges are to make good joints.

5 Open out the top two veneers as shown in Fig 7.10. Join the edges A-A and B-B together to reveal the quartered panel.

6 Assemble the veneers very carefully, ensuring that the figure and joints are accurately aligned, then tape up the joints securely (*see* Fig 7.11).

7 Lay the veneer carefully and accurately.

LAYING THE PANELS

Once made up, with joints securely taped up, book-matched and quartered panels may be laid as for a single sheet (*see* Chapter 5, page 59), or incorporated into another design prior to laying. If cross-banding or an inlay is to be added, this should be done prior to laying, and the panel treated as though it were made up of a single sheet of veneer.

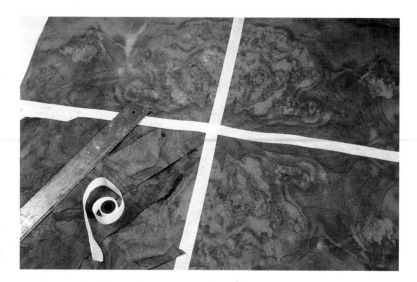

Fig 7.11 A quartered panel, with joints taped, is ready for laying.

INLAYING

- ♦ HISTORY AND TERMINOLOGY
- ♦ TOOLS AND MATERIALS
- ♦ STRINGS AND BANDINGS
- ♦ MARQUETRY MOTIFS

HISTORY AND TERMINOLOGY

The term 'inlay' refers to the technique of inserting wood and other materials (such as metal, mother-of-pearl and plastic) into solid wood groundwork. Historically, a whole range of materials and methods have been used, though inlay work is now generally confined to inserting contrasting wood veneers into a veneer ground. This, and the various names linked to the general technique, has led to some confusion about the term and what it means (*see* Chapter 1).

TOOLS AND MATERIALS

In addition to the veneers, glues and means of pressing the work onto the groundwork, there are some basic tools and materials that will be needed for inlaying strings, bandings and small marquetry motifs: a means of making shallow rebates to accept veneer inlays is needed. Traditionally, this was the scratchstock, but the task is now usually carried out by the portable router. The accuracy with which the depth of cut can be set and the quality of router cutters means that this tool is both quick and reliable. However, the scratchstock should not be disregarded because for intricate work (for example, small veneered boxes), where it may not be easy to set up the router, the scratchstock is ideal. A very sharp bevel-edged chisel is useful for cutting mitres in strings and narrow bandings. Masking tape or Sellotape and veneer pins are needed to secure strings and bandings while preparing built-up patterns.

STRINGS AND BANDINGS

Strings and bandings are available from veneer suppliers in a wide range of designs and widths (*see* Fig 8.1).

Strings are narrow inlay strips of veneer of a single species. They are usually made of boxwood, either in its natural colour or stained black. They are either flat, i.e. simply a narrow strip of veneer, or square in section. Square-sectioned strings are intended to be set into a rebate at the edge of the work (*see* Fig 8.2).

Bandings are made up of two or more species and can be very complex in design, though the feather banding shown in Fig 8.3 relies on the contrasting grain direction of a single species. Bandings are manufactured by gluing solid blocks and veneers together before slicing them into thin strips. While veneer suppliers usually stock a wide range of bandings, there may be occasions when you wish (or need) to make your own. In restoration work, for example, you may find it impossible to track down an exact copy of a missing inlay.

As a general rule, strings and simple bandings are added to create a clear boundary between different parts of a design, such as a central veneer panel and a cross-band, or as a means of relieving a uniform surface. Complex bandings, on the other hand, often provide a decorative effect in their own right.

MAKING STRINGS AND BANDINGS

There is little need to make up your own strings because the range of widths available from veneer suppliers is so good. In fact, it is very difficult to create the narrow strings of $^1/_{16}$in (1.5mm) with any accuracy, and strings are so cheap, it hardly seems

Fig 8.1 Strings and bandings are available from veneer suppliers in a wide range of designs and widths.

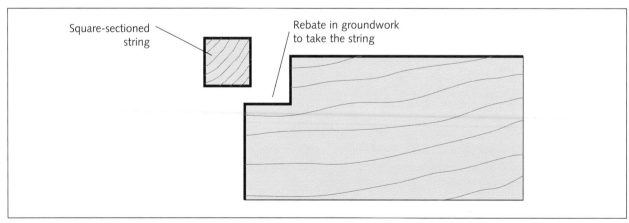

Square-sectioned string

Rebate in groundwork to take the string

Fig 8.2 A square string is intended to be rebated into the edge of a piece of work, acting as a decorative border.

Fig 8.3 Bandings are made up of two or more species, though the feather banding in the middle row uses just one.

Making your own bandings can be something of a challenge, but for restoration work there may be no alternative, as often it isn't possible to buy exact replicas of the missing pieces. The principle is straightforward. Blocks of wood are glued together so that the cross section of the block has the required pattern, and the bandings are produced by slicing the block. (*See* Fig 8.4.) For example, feather banding is produced by gluing together strips of wood that have been cut with the grain on the diagonal. Where the banding is made up of a number of coloured woods or species, the process is obviously more complex, but based on the same principle of gluing blocks of wood together before slicing off the banding on a bandsaw or circular saw (*see* Fig 8.5). The process is quite wasteful in that the width of the cut made by the saw might be greater than the thickness of the inlay! The bandsaw is somewhat less wasteful, but all the same be sure to account for the high wastage when making up the block. After each slice, plane the exposed surface of the block before cutting another banding.

worth the effort. Of course, there may be occasions when you need a width of string that is not readily available, as can happen with restoration work, and you can make up a wider string with relative ease.

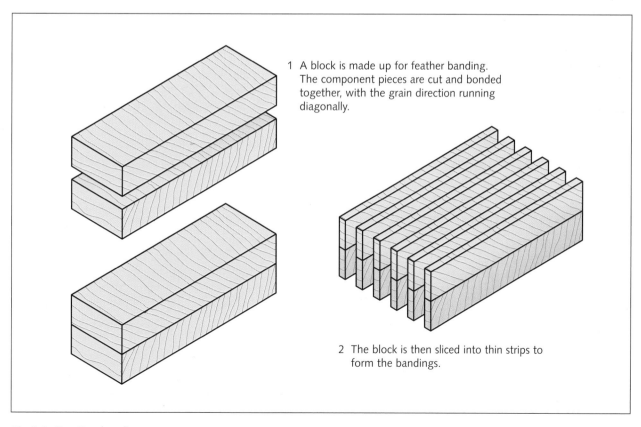

1 A block is made up for feather banding. The component pieces are cut and bonded together, with the grain direction running diagonally.

2 The block is then sliced into thin strips to form the bandings.

Fig 8.4 Creating bandings.

INCORPORATING STRINGS AND BANDINGS

There are two main methods of incorporating a string or banding into a design: they are either incorporated into the pattern before the veneer is laid, or incorporated afterwards by cutting a groove into the laid veneer to take the string or banding.

BEFORE LAYING

Where several pieces of veneer are built up into the final pattern, as with cross-banding, book-matching and quartering, it is probably easier to incorporate the string or banding at the same time. A common approach is to insert the inlay between a cross-band and the main central panel.

The positions of the mitres are marked on the template to ensure that the line of the mitres of the banding and cross-banding match. Strictly speaking, a simple pattern can be built up without the aid of a template, but it is good practice because it encourages good draughtsmanship, and helps you observe the progress of the design as you build it up. For complex patterns, templates are essential. Figure 8.6 shows cross-banding being offered up to a central panel.

To decorate the surfaces of a box, two templates can be used: one for the top face and the second for the front and back faces. For the design shown in Fig 8.7A the string or banding is not positioned around the edge, but directly across the main panel. The templates help to ensure that the bandings are positioned so that they line up across all three faces when laid. The design shown in Fig 8.7B has a wide banding incorporated into the panel to create an effect that is similar to parquetry (*see* Chapter 9), with the main veneer broken up into smaller sections to provide the decorative effect. The main veneer is cut with a veneer knife and straightedge, against the template.

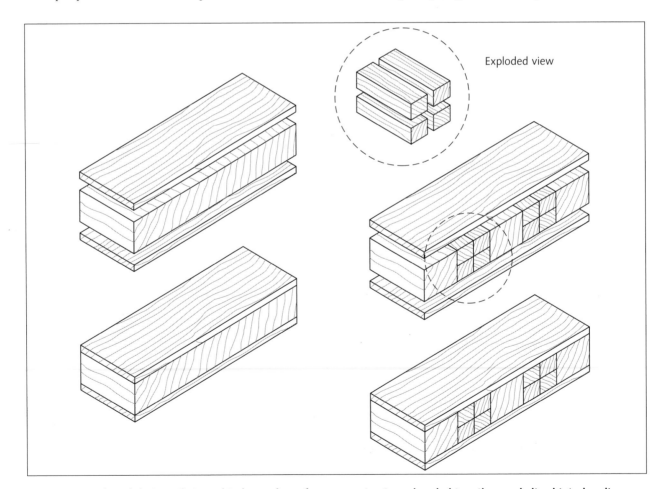

Exploded view

Fig 8.5 Examples of designs that need to be made up from separate pieces bonded together, and sliced into bandings.

Fig 8.6 The cross-banding is offered up to the central panel.

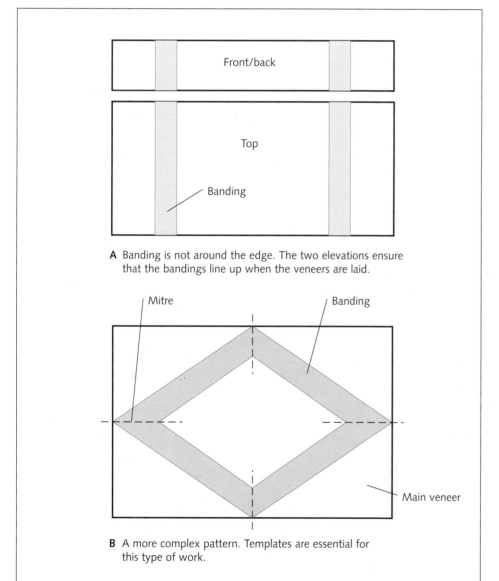

Fig 8.7 Templates for other banding designs.

Front/back

Top

Banding

A Banding is not around the edge. The two elevations ensure that the bandings line up when the veneers are laid.

Mitre

Banding

Main veneer

B A more complex pattern. Templates are essential for this type of work.

One way of building up the patterns shown in Figs 8.7A and 8.7B is to cut the main veneer once at the position of the banding, insert the banding and then bring the other piece of main veneer alongside. However, if you think about this, the figure of the veneer will be displaced by a distance equal to the width of the banding. In some circumstances this may look a little odd, especially if the veneer is highly figured (as with burr or curl) and the banding is wide. It is better to remove a strip of the veneer equal to the width of the banding, using the template as a guide, so that the figure of the main veneer will maintain a continuity across the banding. Veneer pins should be used to hold the main veneer in place on the template while the cuts are made and the joints are assembled and taped. Where mitres are required, the pieces of banding should be overlapped and cut through with the veneer knife, using the guide lines on the template.

Returning to Fig 8.6, the banding, or string, and cross-banding are brought up against the edge of the main veneer and taped in position with the components overlapping at the corners. The mitred joints are made by cutting through all the veneers at each corner, after which they are taped (*see* Fig 8.8). The panel is then ready to lay by press. (*See* Chapter 5.)

SHAPED WORK

This is somewhat more awkward work to deal with. In practice, most strings or bandings used in curved work will be narrow. Clearly, broad inlays are going to be a problem as they will resist being bent to fit. This is especially the case with bandings, which are much more likely to break up as stress is placed on the joints between their component pieces of veneer. Therefore, narrow strings rather than bandings are more likely to be found as inlays in this type of work.

The central panel is prepared and secured on a template as usual. The string is brought up to the edge of the panel and secured with veneer pins pushed into the template, to hold the string against the central panel. Only fairly short sections of the string are brought into contact with the edge at any one time: to attempt the whole length at once could produce too much stress and cause the work to spring open. After the position of the string is secured, the cross-banding or other edge veneer is fitted up against it, and the completed joints are taped. This section of the string is now secure and you can gradually work your way around the rest.

When the string and edge veneer have been taped into place, the built-up pattern can be laid on the groundwork using one of the press methods described in Chapter 5.

Fig 8.8 Cutting the mitres. A single cut makes the best joint.

Fig 8.9 The black string inlay in this highly decorative curl mahogany veneer does not break the continuity of the figure.

AFTER LAYING

The alternative to incorporating the string or banding before laying is to cut a groove in the main veneer after laying and insert the string into the groove before pressing the work again. Figure 8.9 shows the type of work that would suit this approach. The string is laid into the body of the main veneer after laying so that it does not interrupt the continuity of the figure of the main veneer. The groove can be cut by hand, but can be more conveniently, and less laboriously, cut by machine. The portable router makes the work relatively easy, even on shaped work, such as a round table top. For small work, such as a decorative box, the router is not very useful because the working surface is not large enough to support the base of the machine.

An advantage of inserting strings and bandings after laying, is that they can be inlaid into a veneered or solid wood ground. In fact, in the latter case, there would be no other way of carrying out the job. In this sense, the technique is closely related to intarsia work (*see* Chapter 1, page 3).

USING A SCRATCHSTOCK

To form a groove by hand you can use a scratchstock (*see* Chapter 3, page 33). Cutters for this tool are made from old saw blades that are cut, ground or filed to shape. The cutting edge should be the same width as the string or banding. To be sure of the tool, try it out on a piece of scrap wood to check that the string or banding fits the groove. Obviously, it will be too late once you have cut the groove in the work itself only to discover that it is the wrong size or at the wrong distance from the edge. The shape of the cutting edge is worth considering for a moment or two. The tool works by scraping the surface of the wood. Narrow blades can simply be filed square across leaving a small burr on the edge (*see* Fig 8.10A): as the blade scrapes the surface, the burr will help cut the fibres. When the string or banding is a little wider, filing a slight notch into each side will help the blade make a cleaner cut (*see* Fig 8.10B). The slight point that

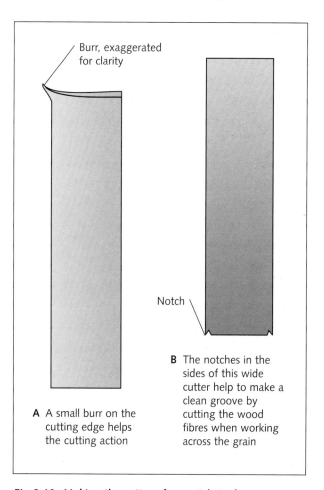

A A small burr on the cutting edge helps the cutting action

B The notches in the sides of this wide cutter help to make a clean groove by cutting the wood fibres when working across the grain

Fig 8.10 Making the cutter of a scratchstock.

this makes at each side of the blade cuts the fibres of the wood when working the tool across the grain.

The blade should be inserted into the stock so that it protrudes enough to cut a groove equal to the thickness of the inlay, and should be positioned at a distance from the fence equal to the distance of the inlay from the edge of the work (*see* Fig 8.11). It is difficult to be accurate in cutting the groove depth, but it is better to err very slightly on too shallow than too deep. In other words, it is better for the inlay to be ever so slightly proud

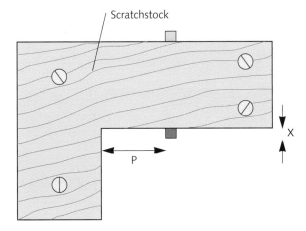

Fig 8.11 Cutter position in the scratchstock. Distance X represents the depth of cut which should equal the inlay thickness, or be very slightly less. Distance P represents the distance of the inlay from the edge of the work.

rather than to sink below the surface. The difference can be removed when sanding the work afterwards. As mentioned before, it is also a good idea to practise on a piece of scrap timber to get it right.

It is also worth noting that if the edge of the work is to be moulded, this should be done *after* the inlay has been laid. If you mould the edge before using the scratchstock, you may make it difficult for the fence of the tool to make a good contact. In other words, the scratchstock may wobble, leading to an untidy, irregular cut.

The position of the inlay needs to be drawn onto the surface to be inlaid, in pencil. This is important, as it shows where the inlay will meet at the corners, so that these positions are not over-shot. The fence is held tight against the edge and the cutter is worked along the surface to create the groove (*see* Fig 8.12). Shavings and dust need to be cleared from the surface at regular intervals to prevent them interfering with the progress of the work. Do not work right into the corners, as it is difficult to make them clean and tidy. Instead, leave a fraction of the surface intact and use a veneer knife or chisel to complete clean, square corners.

A modified scratchstock, as shown in Fig 8.13, is used to cut a groove in circular or oval work. The fence is modified to allow it to work around a curved edge without wobbling. Its width and the two half dowels ensure that it remains stable as it is pressed against the edge of the work (*see* Fig 8.14).

Fig 8.12 Using the scratchstock. Note how the fence is held tight against the edge.

Fig 8.13 A specially made scratchstock for circular work.

It should be noted that for circular or oval work, the inlay will need to be bent to fit the curvature. This means that only very narrow strings or bandings can be used. Wide inlays do not flex easily, and if they do flex, are put under tremendous strain. This puts the bandings at great risk of disintegrating as the adhesive holding the component parts together begins to fail under the pressure.

USING A ROUTER

Modern routers and their cutters are sufficiently versatile to allow very fine work to be undertaken. The depth of cut on many machines can be very finely adjusted, and they are supplied with a parallel fence, enabling them to cut grooves parallel to the edge of the work (*see* Fig 8.15). Among the optional accessories that are available is a trammel bar – this enables a router to cut a circular

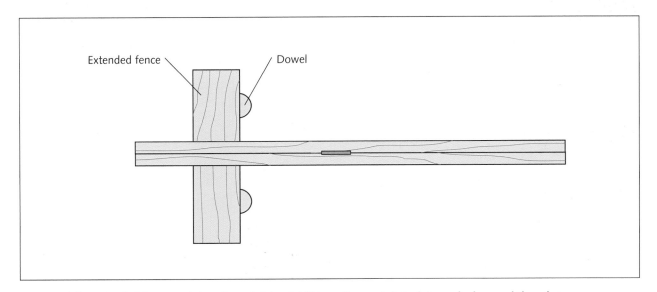

Fig 8.14 The extended fence and dowels maintain stability as the scratchstock is worked around the edge.

Fig 8.15 A router fitted with a parallel fence.

Fig 8.16 A trammel bar fitted to the router for cutting a circular groove.

groove (*see* Fig 8.16). Alternatively, a template can be used to guide the machine as it cuts a groove. For this type of work, the cutters normally employed are straight, single or double fluted, with a bottom cutting edge, for a good, cleanly cut groove. If you are cutting against a template, specially designed cutters with a guide roller are available.

In square or rectangular work, the position of the inlay should be marked in pencil so that the corners can be located, in order to avoid over-shooting them. Use a straight cutter that has the same width as the inlay, and practise on scrap timber to get the depth of cut and distance from the edge absolutely right. When you are satisfied that all is well, cut the groove in the work. You can work right into the corners of the inlay position, but it will have a rounded edge (*see* Fig 8.17). Square off the corner with a veneer knife or chisel (*see* Fig 8.18).

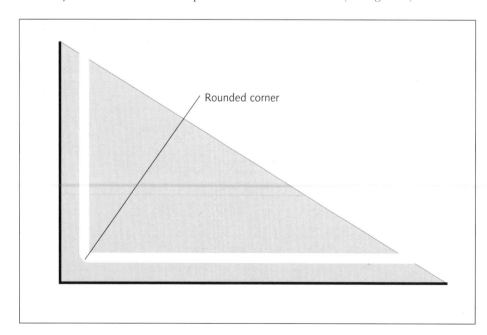

Rounded corner

Fig 8.17 The corners of a groove cut with a router will have a rounded profile.

Shaped work, such as a round or oval table top, presents several possibilities for cutting the groove. The first is to use the trammel bar accessory for the router so that it works like a compass. A template is another possibility, but this is less reliable and needs to be positioned very accurately and anchored to the work in such a way as to avoid damaging the rest of the surface. A template also takes time to make, so is not really appropriate for one-off work. A third option is to modify the parallel fence supplied with the router – Fig 8.19 shows such a modification. The router is fitted with a removable fence that has two rounded pieces of wood (cut from hardwood dowel) glued to the surface: these allow the router to work a groove at a fixed distance from the edge, without rocking over the curve of the edge.

FITTING THE STRING OR BANDING

Only a very small amount of glue is needed for fixing strings or bandings. Too much will prevent them from fitting properly in the groove, and may even prevent narrow strings and bandings from fitting at all, as the glue takes up the available space.

In the case of straight-sided work, such as a square or rectangular table top, the inlay is fitted into the groove one side at a time. The inlay is cut to length by laying it up against the edge of the groove and marking it off. It is easier to pre-cut the mitre as its position in the groove makes cutting it afterwards awkward. Very narrow strings can be mitred freehand with a chisel, but wider strings and bandings will need to have the position of the mitre marked and then be cut accurately with a veneer knife and straightedge. Alternatively, an accurate mitre saw may be used. After brushing on a very thin layer of glue in the groove, press in the inlay

Fig 8.18 Use a veneer knife or chisel to square off the rounded corners.

Fig 8.19 A modified parallel fence for use with the router on circular work.

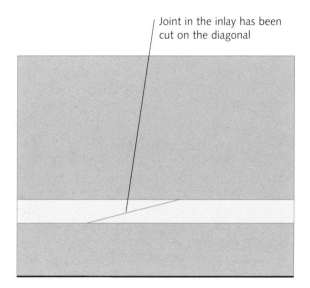

Joint in the inlay has been cut on the diagonal

Fig 8.20 Cutting a joint between adjacent strings diagonally will make it less noticeable.

on the first side. Treat the remaining sides in the same way, fitting each to its neighbour.

With circular work, the process may involve more than one string being fitted because a single piece is often not long enough to complete the circumference. Where this is the case, joints between adjacent strings should be on the diagonal to make them less noticeable (*see* Fig 8.20). This is difficult to achieve at the completion of the circumference when the end meets the beginning, as it were, because you need to make the cut very accurately to prevent a gap from showing. Apart from the last joint that completes the circumference, all the others can be made before the string is placed in the groove.

FITTING SQUARE STRINGS AT AN EDGE

Square-sectioned strings are designed to be fitted to the edge of the work. The contrast between the colour of the string and the rest of the surface gives a very definite and cleanly defined shape to the edge. The technique is frequently applied to boxes, both veneered and non-veneered work.

The string is fitted into a rebate cut into the edge of the work. Where the work is veneered, this should be completed, with the veneer taken right up to the edge before cutting the rebate. Cut the rebate with a rebate plane, a router fitted with a

rebate cutter, or for fitting very small sectioned strings, with a scratchstock. The rebate plane is only suitable for square or rectangular work, but the router and scratchstock can be used on work of any shape.

Figure 8.21 shows how the string is fitted into the rebate. Holding it in place is quite tricky because of the position, but the method illustrated will do the job very well. You can use string or rubber bands, but the simplest and most effective way is with strips of masking tape at regular intervals along the string's length, as shown in Fig 8.21. Where there are corners that are to be rebated, this should be done before fitting.

MARQUETRY MOTIFS

While marquetry and inlaying are really separate techniques, there are occasions when small, ready-made marquetry motifs are incorporated, or 'inlaid', into a plain veneer background. There is a wide range of motifs available from veneer suppliers – Fig 8.22 shows some traditional marquetry designs that can be bought 'off-the-shelf'. They are convenient, but they do take away the challenge of creating your own (*see* Chapter 10).

Fig 8.21 Holding a square string in its rebate while the glue dries.

INCORPORATING MARQUETRY MOTIFS

As with strings and bandings, marquetry motifs can be incorporated into the design either before or after laying.

BEFORE LAYING

This method can only be adopted if the veneers are to be laid using a press. Hammer veneering techniques are not appropriate because of the need to build up the pattern in advance. The motif, or any template that may be supplied with it, is carefully positioned on the main veneer and the outline marked with a veneer knife. The waste veneer is then cut away and the motif fitted into the space and taped in place. A built-up pattern is laid using one of the press methods described in Chapter 5.

AFTER LAYING

You may prefer to lay the main veneers first and add the motifs afterwards. This is the usual technique where the main veneers have been laid using the hammer method, and the only technique where motifs are added to an already existing veneered surface.

The motif is marked out on the main veneer and a knife used to cut through the veneer. Clearly, the waste cannot be simply lifted out, and it is necessary to carefully remove the waste with sharp chisels. If you are very careful and confident using a router, you can remove most of the waste with it and then clean up around the edges with the chisel. After the waste has been removed, the motif can be glued into position and the joint taped before applying pressure in a press or with cauls.

Fig 8.22 Examples of marquetry inlay motifs.

PARQUETRY AND OYSTER WORK

THE NATURE OF PARQUETRY

Some of the most exciting decorative effects with veneer have been created using strongly contrasting grain configurations of a single species of wood rather than contrasting colours. Traditional parquetry is the use of veneer in geometric shapes, in which varying grain directions of the component pieces reflect light in different ways, creating areas of light and dark which change as the viewer's position changes. Other parquetry effects incorporate colour differences as well, the classic example being the chessboard design. The shapes most commonly associated with parquetry are squares, rectangles and diamonds.

Because the technique involves the principle of tessellation, i.e. the repeated use of geometric shapes that fit together without any gaps, there are two major principles that need to be observed. The first is the need for good draughtsmanship, and the second, the need for consummate care in cutting the shapes accurately. Not all shapes will tessellate – they must first satisfy some basic conditions of geometry. This is where good draughtsmanship comes into its own, and as a matter of good practice, a template should be marked out. This not only provides a base upon which to build the design prior to laying, it also gives you the opportunity to check that the design will work before you start cutting veneer.

The important point to remember with parquetry is that its success depends very much on the accuracy of cutting angles. The work is usually repetitive (i.e. you cut fairly large numbers of the same shape and size components) and the task of cutting these accurately is made much easier with the aid of parquetry jigs (*see* page 34). The need for great accuracy in making the jigs cannot be over-emphasized. Any errors in their construction will be compounded when the component veneers are built up into the pattern. The two critically important factors in successful parquetry are:

● accurate cutting of angles, which is achieved by the careful use of accurately made jigs; and

● taking time to consider the direction of the grain in the veneer sheet relative to the way it is cut to make the component shapes.

With respect to the second point, it is worth spending some time practising cutting the pattern out of paper with the grain direction marked on to see just how the grain pattern in the main sheets of veneer should be aligned before you commit yourself to cutting the veneer itself. What may work in your head may not work in practice because of some geometrical quirk that you did not think about.

Figure 9.1 shows a design that I used some years ago to replace the missing leaf of a dining table. I drew up the template to check a number of details, marking the position of the cross-banding and the string first, and then the diamonds. The particular problem that needed to be solved was how to match up the diamonds on the leaf with those on the two D-ends so that when the table was fully open, the diamonds showed a continuity across the whole surface. The template provided an opportunity to determine how this could be achieved.

The main shapes that tessellate easily are squares and rectangles, and triangles and diamonds where the angles are either 60° or 120° (*see* Figs 9.2A and 9.2B). The essential test for tessellation is indicated in Fig 9.2D. If all the angles around point X add up to 360°, then tessellation is possible. Most parquetry involves the use of regular shapes, such as those illustrated in Fig 9.2. It is also possible to combine different shapes, but you need to draw the pattern to ensure that the design works and then to recreate accurately the shapes you have drawn.

SQUARES AND RECTANGLES

The easiest shapes to work with are squares and rectangles. They are relatively easy shapes to cut accurately and they tessellate well. The typical example of this work is the traditional chessboard design. There are, of course, many other possible combinations of squares and rectangles.

CHESSBOARD AND BASKET WEAVE DESIGNS

The traditional chessboard design uses alternating squares of contrasting woods – light and dark (*see* Fig 9.3). Basket weave designs use squares of the same species, and therefore colour, but with the grain direction of adjacent squares alternating (*see* Fig 9.4).

At first sight, the method of construction appears to involve fitting together the individual squares,

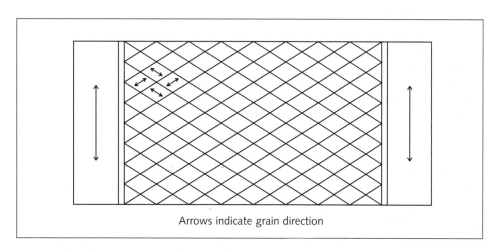

Arrows indicate grain direction

Fig 9.1 This design was a template used to reconstruct the missing leaf of a dining table.

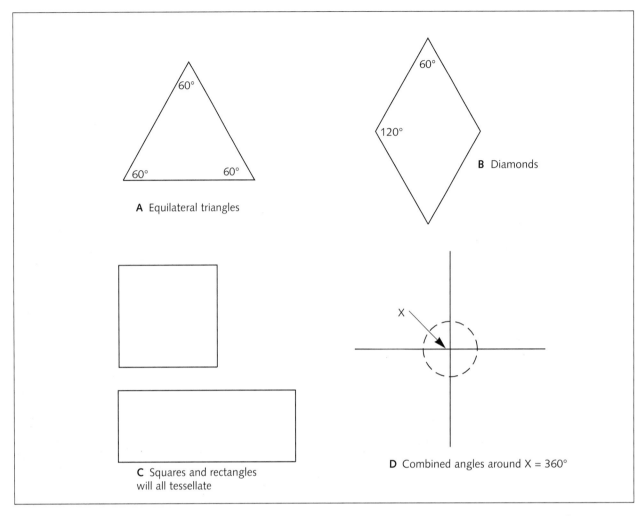

A Equilateral triangles

B Diamonds

C Squares and rectangles will all tessellate

D Combined angles around X = 360°

Fig 9.2 **The fundamental condition of tessellation is that the combined angles of all the sides at the point of contact, indicated by X, is 360°.**

Fig 9.3 **Traditional chessboard design using squares of contrasting colours.**

Fig 9.4 **This 'basket weave' effect is generated by using squares of the same species, but with alternating grain direction.**

but this is probably neither the best nor the most efficient way of doing it. A better way to build up the pattern is to cut parallel strips of veneer, join them together, and then cut across in the opposite direction to create new strips of joined squares. (*See* Figs 9.5 to 9.8.)

A simple jig will aid the cutting of parallel veneer strips. Figure 9.9 shows such a jig in use. The straightedge is held against the two spacers (in this instance, coins), which keeps it parallel to the fence. The spacers must be of a width equal to the size of the squares. The first job, however, is to trim the edge of the veneer on a shooting board so that it is straight and butts tight against the fence of the jig. Once this is done, the veneer strips can be

Fig 9.5 Shooting the edge of the assembled strips that will butt against the fence on the cutting jig.

Fig 9.6 Cutting the strips of squares.

Fig 9.7 Assembling the strips to form the design of alternating squares.

Fig 9.8 The finished designs. Left: A typical chessboard design in mahogany and sycamore. Right: A basket weave pattern in mahogany.

Fig 9.9 Cutting parallel strips of veneer using the jig.

cut with one stroke of the knife, which should be held vertically. After cutting each strip, the exposed edge of the main sheet of veneer should be planed on the shooting board, just in case it is not exactly true. This will minimize errors caused by a possible loss of squareness.

As the shooting board is used several times during the process, and surplus squares must be removed after the final assembly, enough veneer to allow for this wastage, and for the inevitable human error that creeps in, must be included.

CREATING A CHESSBOARD DESIGN

1 Cut parallel strips of light and dark coloured veneers.

2 Tape the strips together, alternating light and dark veneers (*see* Fig 9.10A). If you use good quality, clear cellulose tape, such as Sellotape, you will be able to see the joints, which will help you later when fitting the whole design together.

3 Cut the assembled veneers into parallel strips, this time cutting at right angles to the joints after first truing up the edge that will be placed against the fence of the jig. The end result is a series of strips, each with alternating light and dark squares. (*See* Fig 9.10B.)

4 Line the strips up to form a chessboard pattern and tape them together (*see* Fig 9.10C). You should now see why clear tape is helpful in aligning the joints accurately. You will need one square more on each strip than will be used in the final design, because each line will include one square that will be wasted.

5 Trim off the surplus squares and true all the sides on a shooting board to prepare the pattern for incorporation into the overall design.

6 Finally, lay the assembled pattern following one of the methods given in Chapter 5.

CREATING A BASKET WEAVE DESIGN

1 Cut the veneers (usually of a single species) into strips.

2 Tape the strips together, so that alternate strips have the grain direction running along their length and across their width respectively, as shown in Fig 9.11A.

3 Cut the assembled veneers into parallel strips, cutting at right angles to the joints, to produce a series of strips with squares of alternating grain direction.

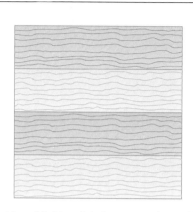

A Cut strips of light and dark veneers, the width of each being equal to the sides of the chessboard squares, then tape alternate strips together.

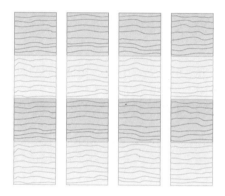

B Cut the assembled work into new strips, cutting at right angles to the original cuts. The resultant strips will be made up of individual squares.

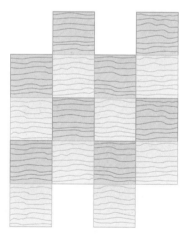

C Line the strips up and tape them together to form the familiar chessboard pattern. Note that there is one extra square at the end of each line caused by the lining up process.

Fig 9.10 Creating a chessboard design.

A Cut strips of veneer of different grain direction (the two being at right angles to each other), but of equal width. Tape the alternate strips together.

B Cut the assembled work into new strips, cutting at right angles to the original cuts. Line the new strips up and tape them to form a pattern of squares of alternating grain direction. There will be one extra square at the end of each line.

Fig 9.11 Creating a basket weave design.

4 Reassemble the strips by shifting each one along one square (*see* Fig 9.11B). Again, this will produce a waste square at the end of each row.

5 Trim away the surplus squares before shaving all four sides square on the shooting board.

6 Lay the assembled veneer following one of the methods given in Chapter 5.

DIAMONDS

The use of 60°/120° diamonds is very common in parquetry work, with triangles used a little less. Much of the effect they generate relies on the interplay of light and alternating grain direction: Fig 9.12 illustrates a similar effect to that seen in the basket weave pattern described in the last section, using alternating grain direction. In fact, apart from the obvious need to work out how to cut the veneer at appropriate angles, the method of construction is similar. The effect illustrated in Fig 9.13, on the other hand, is a little more laborious. The impact of this cube design is

stunning. Individual diamonds are fitted together to generate two optical illusions: one, that the pattern is a series of cubes and the second, that the orientation of these cubes changes as you look at them.

ALTERNATING GRAIN DESIGN

The principle of setting out a template for the design is advisable here. Grain directions can be marked in (*see* Fig 9.14) and it helps with estimating the number of strips needed to make the design, which tends to be harder with diamonds than with squares.

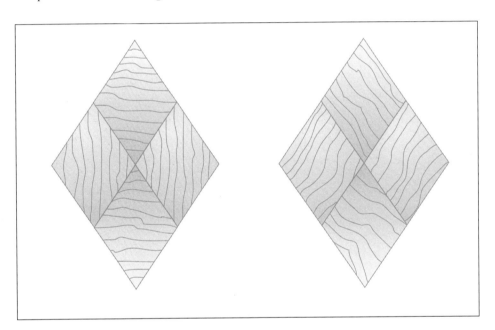

Fig 9.12 Diamonds arranged with alternating grain direction.

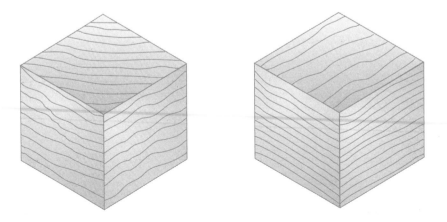

Fig 9.13 The cube pattern appears very spectacular over a larger surface.

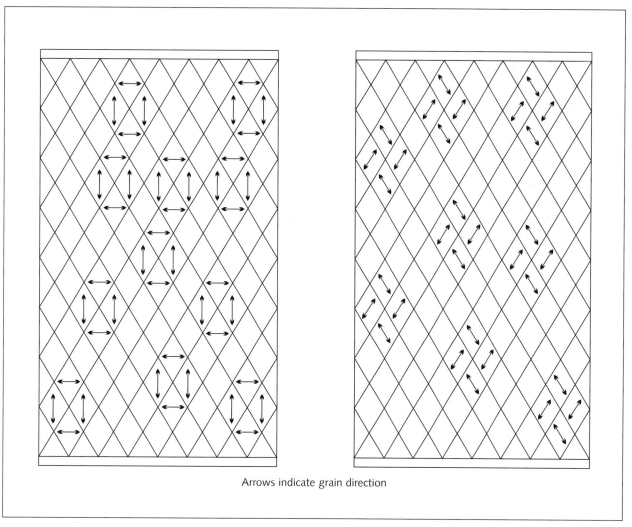

Arrows indicate grain direction

Fig 9.14 Template designs for different grain configurations in diamond patterns. Note that the grain direction is not necessarily recorded in every diamond, but in sufficient number to form a good reference.

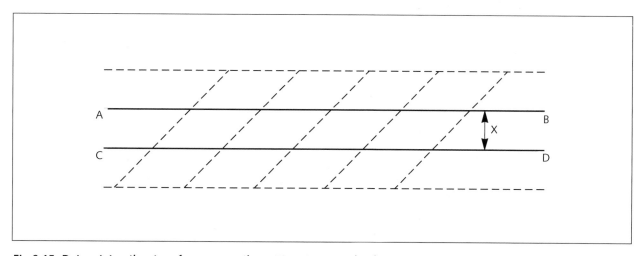

Fig 9.15 Determining the size of spacers on the cutting jig – X is the distance required.

The tools required to make diamonds are the shooting board and parallel cutting jig, as for squares. There are, however, a couple of important modifications. First of all, the shooting board will need a temporary diamond planing fence. Secondly, the spacers for the parallel cutting jig do not represent the length of the sides of the diamond, but the distance between the parallel sides of it (*see* Fig 9.15). Sides A-B and C-D are parallel to each other in the diamond, so the perpendicular distance between them, X, is the size required for the spacers.

The next problem concerns the orientation of the grain and how this relates to the cutting and assembling of the strips. The grain runs parallel to the length and at 60° to the width, and parallel to the length and at right angles to the width, in alternate strips (*see* Fig 9.16).

A pattern of diamonds with alternating grain direction can be created in two ways. One way is to draw the design on a template, and to cut individual diamonds, fitting and taping them together on the template as you go. A simpler, less laborious method is given below.

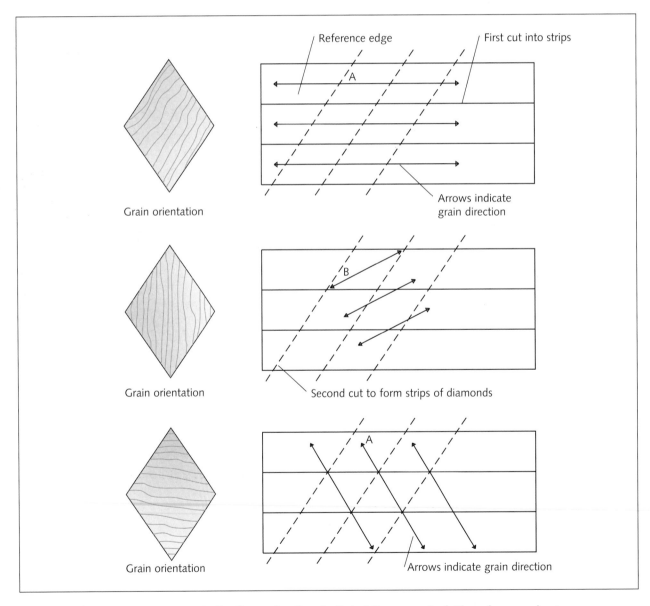

Fig 9.16 Relating grain orientation in the diamond pattern to that of the veneer leaf. The reference edge is trued up so that when the second cuts are made to the taped-up strips, A will be 60°, B will be 30°.

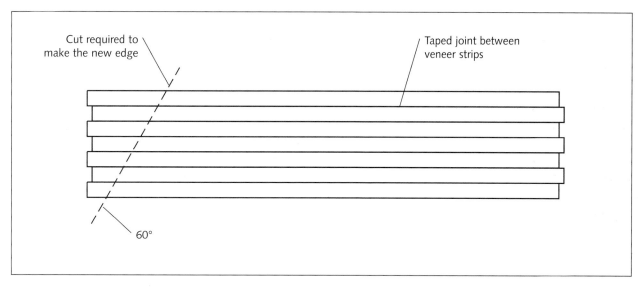

Fig 9.17 A new edge is cut at 60° to the taped joints and trued up on the shooting board.

CREATING A DIAMOND PATTERN WITH ALTERNATING GRAIN

1 Cut parallel strips of veneer, using the cutting jig. The first cut in the veneer leaf creates a reference edge that sets the direction of the grain in the strips. This edge should be trued up on the shooting board, using a temporary fence, so that the angles marked A in Fig 9.16 are exactly 60°. Plane the edge of the leaf true in this way after each strip is cut.

2 Place the strips together, with their grain direction alternating, and secure them with clear cellulose tape.

3 Cut a new edge between the strips, at an angle of 60° to the joints (*see* Fig 9.17). Plane this smooth on the shooting board, using the temporary fence to ensure accuracy.

4 Return the assembled strips to the cutting jig and cut strips of diamonds as shown in Fig 9.18.

5 Fit strips together on the template to make up the design.

6 Once the design is assembled, lay the veneer (*see* Chapter 5).

Fig 9.18 Cutting strips of diamonds.

THE CUBE

The striking optical effect of the cube design is created by fitting together individual diamonds rather than strips of diamonds. This makes the work more laborious when decorating large areas, but the effort is rewarded! There are two main tasks involved in creating a cube design; cutting individual diamonds, and assembling the pattern. A template is required for assembling this design (*see* Fig 9.19).

CREATING A CUBE DESIGN

1 Make up a template for the design, with the pattern of diamonds drawn on it.

2 Before cutting the diamonds, work out the grain direction (*see* Fig 9.16). Figure 9.20 shows cubes constructed with variations in the grain direction.

3 Cut the diamonds either individually, or in strips. If cut in strips, the diamonds must then be separated for assembly.

4 Assemble the cubes on the template. This may be done in one of two ways. The first is to assemble each individual cube, and then to fit these together on the template (*see* Fig 9.21). The second is to assemble the whole pattern by fitting the diamonds individually. This second method carries an increased risk of error because of the differing orientations of the diamonds. Any slight error in the fitting of one diamond throws out the fitting of

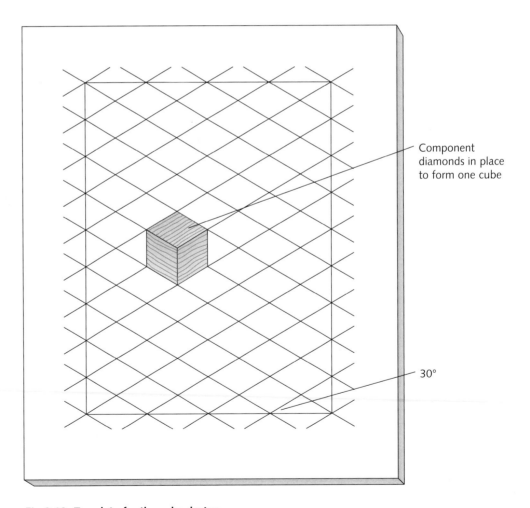

Component diamonds in place to form one cube

30°

Fig 9.19 Template for the cube design.

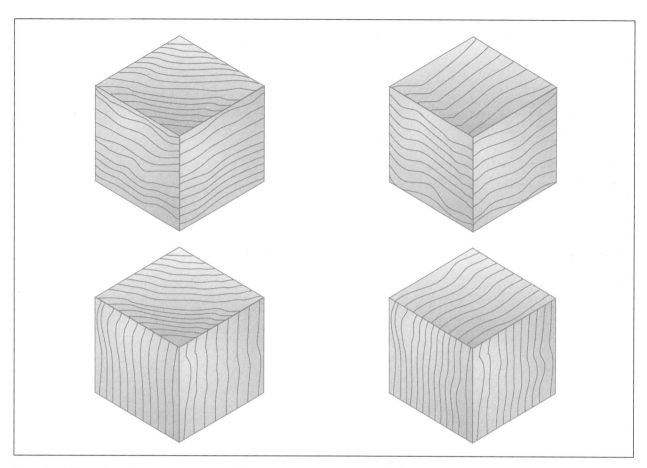

Fig 9.20 Different grain configurations can be used to create a variety of effects.

Fig 9.21 Assembling cubes to make up the design.

Fig 9.22 Cube design completely assembled, trimmed, and fitted with cross-banding, ready for laying.

the rest of the design, so great care is needed in the assembly.

5 Lay the assembled veneer following one of the methods given in Chapter 5.

VARIATIONS

There are many variations on basic parquetry designs, which can be achieved by adapting the basic techniques. As your experience grows, you may wish to experiment with different designs: the advantage of working with veneers is that they are relatively inexpensive, so the cost of mistakes should not inhibit experimentation. The underlying secret of success in creating new designs is the template. A full-scale drawing of the work is essential to test the viability of the design. The following examples give an idea of what can be done.

SQUARES AND RECTANGLES

In Fig 9.23, squares are assembled to create a diamond design, and this idea is further extended in Fig 9.24, where each square is bounded by cross-

Fig 9.23 Squares assembled to resemble a diamond pattern.

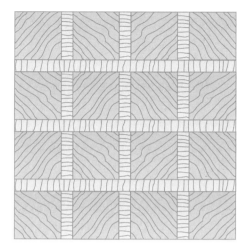

Fig 9.24 Squares bounded by cross-grained strips.

Fig 9.26 Use of equilateral triangles.

banding made of rectangles and long strips of veneer. To assemble this design, each square is fitted individually, with the cross-grained strips added as the work progresses. The template helps to show how the work should be assembled. For example, it can be seen that one long, cross-grained strip might be positioned on the template first, with each square placed against it in turn. The shorter cross-grained strips might then be fitted either side of a square before the next square is put into position, and so on until the design is complete.

The design in Fig 9.25 looks difficult because each square is bounded by a narrow string. The assembly of this is not as awkward as it might appear – it is a variation of the chessboard design (*see* page 108). After the first set of parallel strips are cut, they are assembled as in Fig 9.5, but with

a string placed between the adjacent strips. When this assembly is cut into strips and reassembled to make the final design (as in Fig 9.7), an intervening string is placed between the adjacent strips, so that each square is automatically bounded by a string.

DIAMONDS

Figure 9.26 shows a pattern based on equilateral triangles, each of which is half of a 60°/120° diamond. Each triangle has to be added individually. Where components are added individually to a design, there is the risk of compounding error, as stated earlier. It is therefore necessary to monitor how everything is fitting as it is assembled, and, if necessary, to make any adjustments along the way, using the template as a guide.

The patterns shown in Figs 9.27 and 9.28 use diamonds, with intervening strings and cross-grained strips of veneer. These can be tackled in a similar way to the squares with strips and strings shown in Figs 9.24 and 9.25.

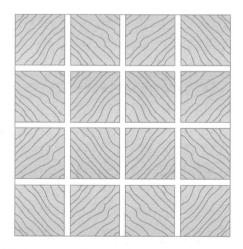

Fig 9.25 Squares outlined with strings.

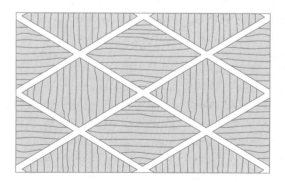

Fig 9.27 Diamonds surrounded by strings.

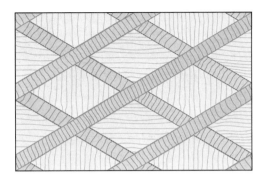

Fig 9.28 Diamonds surrounded by cross-grained veneers.

Provided you take the trouble to prepare drawings to check the ability of the shapes in your design to tessellate, you have a free hand to experiment. You may even experiment with different shapes in the same design. A good example of this is using octagons, which do not normally tessellate, interspersed with small squares to enable tessellation.

OYSTER WORK

Oysters can be obtained from veneer suppliers, but they can be made relatively easily in your own workshop from narrow diameter trunks. Laburnum is frequently used because of the strongly contrasting colours that make up its annual rings: it is the ring pattern that gives the name oyster to this type of veneer.

If you do make your own oysters, you will need to take precautions against the effects of shrinkage as they dry out. If an oyster dries out too quickly it will twist and split, as the rings separate like those of an onion. Oysters are usually about $\frac{1}{8}$in (3mm) thick and can be cut from the unseasoned log by a circular saw or bandsaw, but they must be stored with great care to ensure that they dry out slowly and remain flat. The cut may be directly across the log, or at an angle to create an oval shape. An angled cut reduces the risk of the oyster splitting or distorting. Newly cut oysters can be stacked and weighted to keep them flat, with absorbent paper laid between each piece. They should be stored in a cool, dark place, for several months. Even so, you may need to patch defects that were present at the time of cutting, or that have arisen as a result of the drying process.

The natural shapes of oysters will not tessellate, so they need to be trimmed to shapes that will. The easiest shapes are squares and rectangles (*see* Fig 9.29), of course, but there are alternatives, such as hexagons. Unlike knife-cut veneers though, they cannot be trimmed effectively with a veneer knife. This is where the veneer saw comes into its own. Use the saw to trim the oyster, giving it roughly straight sides (*see* Fig 9.30), before accurately shaping and truing up the edges on the shooting board. The pattern can then be assembled and securely taped prior to laying.

Fig 9.29 Oysters squared-up for tessellation.

Fig 9.30 Trimming oyster veneer to make a hexagon shape. This shape tessellates perfectly.

HANDLING ASSEMBLED VENEERS

There is a general point to be made about the fragility of assembled veneers. Veneers are fragile materials that require careful handling and storage. Assembled veneers need particular care and attention when being transferred to the groundwork. It is better to make the transfer distance very short: in other words, have the assembled veneer with the item to be veneered nearby. Large areas of veneer should be transferred with the assistance of a helper, to reduce flexing and the possibility of misplacement.

FINAL POINTS TO CONSIDER

Many parquetry designs rely on the effect they have on the way light is reflected rather than on real colour differences between component veneers.

Therefore, you always need to consider the position from which the design will be viewed. If a design is being repeated on different faces of the work (e.g. different sides of a box, on a matching pair of doors, or on two or more drawer fronts), you must ensure that the panels are built up and laid with the grain configurations correctly positioned. It is very easy to make the mistake of not matching grain configuration. This error may not appear too bad just after laying, but when a polish is applied it will become glaringly obvious in its optical effects.

The process of building up the veneers into a pattern of many component pieces requires a great deal of tape to hold the joints together. If the tape is stretched while it is being applied to the joints, you may find that the panel will not lie flat because joints are put under tension, and this could prove to be a problem when laying the panel. Make sure you do not stretch the tape when you apply it. Remaining with the subject of tape, it is also very easy to end up with a surface that is tape bound – i.e. has tape in many layers – so don't overdo it. Use only enough tape to secure the joints.

10

MARQUETRY

♦ THE NATURE OF MARQUETRY

♦ TOOLS AND MATERIALS

♦ THE WINDOW METHOD

♦ SAND SHADING

♦ MULTIPLE PIECES AND REPEATED DESIGNS

♦ INCORPORATING A MARQUETRY PANEL

♦ THE MACHINE FRETSAW

♦ ADDING A BORDER AND LAYING

THE NATURE OF MARQUETRY

There are similarities between marquetry and parquetry. In certain types of marquetry, the dividing line between the two techniques is very fine. Marquetry is generally regarded as 'pictures in wood', and this is a pretty good way of distinguishing between the use of geometrical shapes to produce repeated patterns, as in parquetry, and the freer form of design in marquetry.

Marquetry developed from the technique of intarsia (*see* Chapter 1, page 3). This true inlay involved inserting pieces of wood, or other decorative material, into a contrasting groundwork to make up a pictorial design. Marquetry, a highly specialized area of veneering, has developed its

principles and methods to a very high level of skill. An example is shown in Fig 10.1.

TOOLS AND MATERIALS

The only tool that is specific to marquetry, and not usually a part of other veneering techniques, is the fretsaw. All else is much the same, including knives, straightedges and shooting boards. Marquetry embraces a technique known as the 'window method', and this relies upon the accurate use of the veneer knife: Fig 10.2 shows a knife whose design many marquetry workers prefer because of the ease with which it can be manipulated when cutting tight curves or delicate shapes. For the more

Fig 10.1 A marquetry panel that would normally be cut with a fretsaw.

THE WINDOW METHOD

Figure 10.3 shows a marquetry panel used to decorate the top of a small box. As it was a one-off project, the window method was used to make it. The general principle behind this method is that design details cut into the background veneer provide a hole, or window, through which outlines are marked on the detail veneer. When the detail is cut, using the marked line as a guide, this piece should fit neatly into the space created for it. In a sense, it is template work in reverse. An advantage of this method is that when the detail veneer is positioned beneath the window, it can be moved around to orientate the grain pattern and direction in the way you want.

CREATING SIMPLE DESIGNS

complex pictures, using the window method, thin card (referred to as 'waster' card) is needed to form a template for forming the window, and carbon paper is needed for tracing the design onto the veneer.

For the purposes of illustration, the method given below follows the creation of the design shown in Fig 10.3. This is a relatively simple design in that there is a single background veneer into which all the detail will be cut, with the string and border added later.

Fig 10.2 This knife is of a design preferred by many 'marquetrarians'. Its handle shape makes it easier to manipulate the blade around tight curves.

Fig 10.3 A marquetry picture that would normally be constructed using the window method.

1 Create a drawing of the design. I use good quality white paper, and mark in a series of numbers and arrows on each part of the diagram (*see* Figs 10.4 and 10.5). The arrows represent intended grain direction, while the numbers are a code for the species of veneer, linked to a separate numbered list of the veneers to be used.

2 Tape the design securely to the background veneer, along one edge, so that it lies flat on the surface and can be lifted over like a flap. All veneers must be absolutely flat. Any undulation in the surface will lead to badly fitting joints.

It is good practice to make registration marks, as shown in Fig 10.5, so that the design can be placed in exactly the same place if it is removed. While the simplicity of this particular design does not require it, complex panels with a lot of detail do, because the detail is not all drawn in at the same time, but added as you build up the work.

3 Trace the design lightly onto the veneer with carbon paper, including the boundary between the

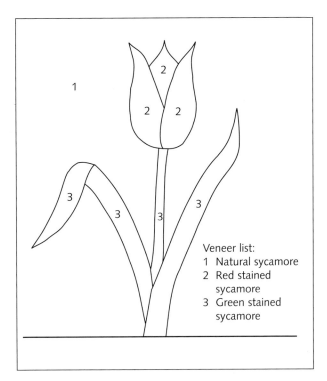

Veneer list:
1 Natural sycamore
2 Red stained sycamore
3 Green stained sycamore

Fig 10.4 The drawing used to create the box lid panel shown in Fig 10.3, noting species of veneer.

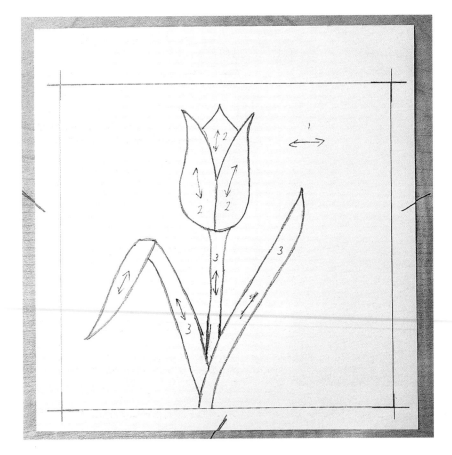

Fig 10.5 Tape the design onto the background veneer. Note the registration marks that will allow accurate relocation of the design on the veneer.

background veneer and any border veneer, though there is no need to trace in the border.

4 Lift over the drawing and cut one of the component parts very carefully. (With simple designs such as this, there is no particular cutting order for the parts.) Keep the knife blade vertical and follow the outline. Where the lines are not straight, it is difficult to cut through with one stroke, so you will need two or three careful cuts, ensuring that you keep to the original line of cut. For long cuts or gentle curves, the knife can be held at 45° to the surface, but for short cuts and sharp curves, it must be near vertical (*see* Fig 10.6).

Very tight curves are best dealt with in a slightly different way. Rather than cut the outline with strokes, it is more effective to make a series of piercing actions with the point of the knife blade. This is especially important if the veneer is hard or brittle.

To prevent fragile edges on these tight curves from splintering out, place Sellotape over the veneer.

5 Remove this first piece from the background, and position the appropriate detail veneer under the window thus formed. Move the detail veneer around to find the grain pattern and direction that you want. Using the point of the blade, mark the outline of the window on the detail veneer. Hold the blade vertically, and move it around the outline, right up against the edge.

6 Take the detail veneer out from under the background, and cut out the shape, carefully working around the scored line. Place the piece into the window made for it. If it has been well cut, the fit will be good; if the fit is poor, with very obvious gaps, discard the piece, and cut another.

7 Turn the work over and rub a little PVA glue over the joints to hold the veneer in its window.

8 Continue this process of cutting out the shape of each component from the background veneer, marking the outline of the window on the detail veneer, and cutting out and inserting the components in their respective windows, until the design is complete. Each time a piece is inserted into its window, rub a little PVA into the back of the joint to set it in place.

9 Trim the finished design on the shooting board and fit a border if required (*see* Chapter 6).

CREATING COMPLEX DESIGNS

Complex designs, in which the background may be made up of two or more veneers, require a different approach from simple designs. A complex panel is built up by cutting out and fitting together the background first. Once this is done, the foreground

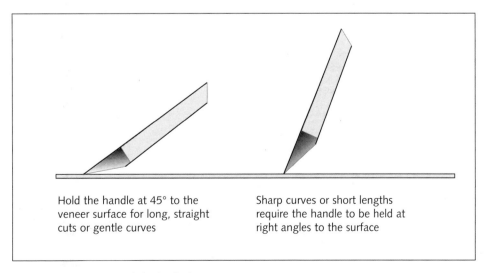

Hold the handle at 45° to the veneer surface for long, straight cuts or gentle curves

Sharp curves or short lengths require the handle to be held at right angles to the surface

Fig 10.6 Correct use of the knife for marquetry.

is then built up. The work is planned in layers, according to the levels of detail. The first layer of detail is the background, the second the main foreground elements, and any subsequent layers are details which are positioned 'on top of' these main foreground elements (*see* Figs 10.7 to 10.10). The more detail there is in a picture, the greater the number of layers required. The process depends not only on the worker being skilled with the knife, but also on being able to organize the work successfully into different layers.

The method given below follows the development of the design shown in Fig 10.11. For this process a sheet of thin card, known as a 'waster', is required.

1 Draw the background design onto good quality white paper, marking in numbers and arrows to indicate the grain direction and veneers used for each piece (*see* Fig 10.12).

2 Tape this design onto a sheet of thin card (the waster) along one edge, so that it lies flat on the waster and can be lifted over like a flap (*see* Fig 10.12). Make sure that the waster is absolutely flat to minimize the risk of badly fitting joints.

3 Trace the background design onto the waster, making the border slightly oversize to allow for trimming later. (Figure 10.13 shows the elements of the sample design that form the background.) Draw in some registration marks so that the drawing can be repositioned accurately when cutting successive windows as the foreground is built up.

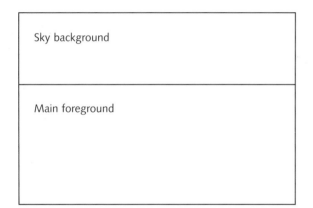

Fig 10.7 A marquetry design is built up in stages. The background veneers are tackled first.

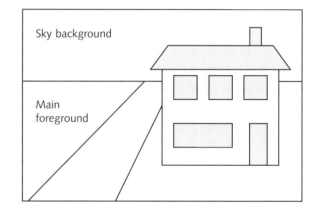

Fig 10.9 The third level of detail is the windows and doors, which are cut into the house veneers.

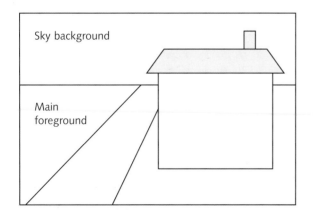

Fig 10.8 For this design, the next level of detail is the house shape and road cut into the background.

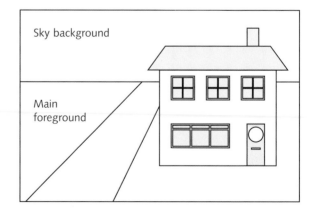

Fig 10.10 The fourth level is the window panes which are cut into the window veneers.

Fig 10.11 A marquetry design that is more complex and requires several stages in its production. The background is made up of several veneers.

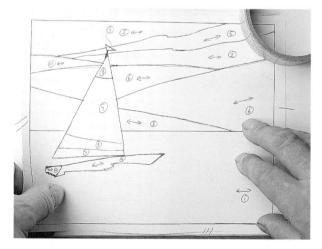

Fig 10.12 Taping the drawing to the waster card so that it is hinged at the top to lift over. Note the registration marks to allow accurate realignment of the design.

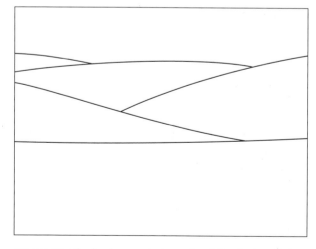

Fig 10.13 The background elements of the design that are traced onto the waster card.

4 Lift over the drawing to reveal the tracing on the waster. For complex designs with background and foreground pieces, a definite cutting order must be followed: cutting must begin with the most distant point (as regards perspective), and then work towards the closest. In this design, the most distant point is the sky (*see* Fig 10.14).

5 Position the veneer to be used for the sky under the window created, manipulating it until you align the grain and figure that you desire, and score the outline of the window onto the veneer surface.

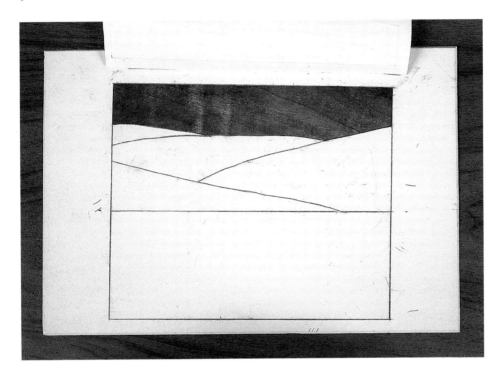

Fig 10.14 Cutting out the sky leaves a window for the appropriate veneer.

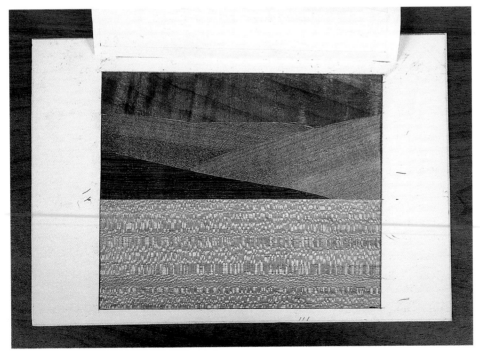

Fig 10.15 With the background veneers in position, the waster card acts as a temporary border.

6 Remove the sky veneer, cut the shape from it, and fit it into the window. Turn the card over and rub a little PVA glue along the boundary between the veneer and the card.

7 In the same way, cut and fit into the waster card, the remaining veneers that make up the background, working from those areas farthest away in the picture, to those nearest the viewer. Rub a little PVA glue into the underside of each joint to hold the pieces in place. (*See* Fig 10.15.) The waster card acts as a temporary border.

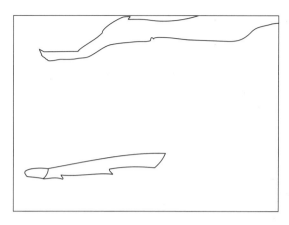

Fig 10.16 The main elements of the foreground design that is traced onto the background.

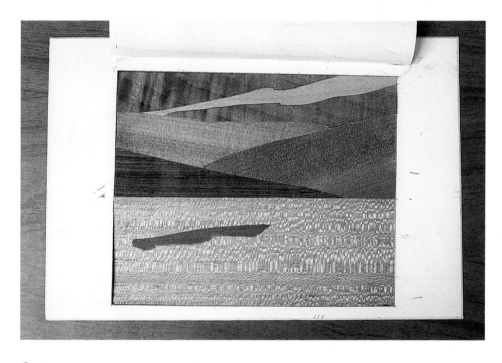

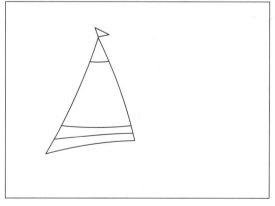

Fig 10.17 The end result after replacing the traced pattern with veneers.

8 Reposition the drawing so that the registration marks are aligned perfectly, and trace the main foreground onto the background veneers. (Figure 10.16 shows the elements of the design that will be traced.)

9 Again starting with the most distant point, cut windows into the background veneer, trace through these onto the appropriate foreground veneers, cut out the foreground pieces, position them in their respective windows, and rub a little PVA into the underside of the joints. (Figure 10.17 shows the veneers in place.)

Fig 10.18 The next level of detail is traced onto the background veneers.

Fig 10.19 The completed design.

10 Begin the process again with the next level of detail (*see* Fig 10.18), tracing the pieces onto the veneers, cutting windows, and then cutting and inserting the pieces. (Figure 10.19 shows the completed design.)

SAND SHADING

Some marquetry designs include pieces of veneer that appear to have darker edges. These shaded pieces of veneer produce the same illusion an artist creates when shading in a pencil or line drawing – it gives a sense of depth and three dimensionality. (*See* Fig 10.20.)

The effect is created by scorching the veneer in hot silver sand. The technique, known as 'sand shading', takes a little time to master – and perhaps quite a few pieces of veneer burnt to ash – but it does give a lift to designs.

To shade veneer, place some clean, dry sand on a metal plate, and heat it over a low heat, on a gas or electric ring. It is very easy to overheat the sand and reduce the veneer to charcoal! Heat the sand on a low heat and test it with some scrap veneer to ensure it is not too hot before you risk shading the painstakingly cut marquetry component. When you are sure that the temperature is right, quickly dip

the edge of the veneer into the hot sand. Some experimentation with scrap veneer may be needed to determine how far you should dip it into the sand to get the desired effect. A classic example of how sand shading enhances a work is shown in Fig 10.20; without this, the marquetry panel would be very flat and uninspiring.

Silver sand is easily obtained from garden nurseries, packaged in relatively small amounts, for example $4\frac{1}{2}$lb (2kg). You won't need a great deal of it. Red sand should not be used because of the risk of staining the veneer, particularly with light-coloured species.

Fig 10.20 Sand shading.

MULTIPLE PIECES AND REPEATED DESIGNS

Where repeated designs are required, the fretsaw provides the ideal means of cutting identical components. Figure 10.21 shows an identical repeated design that is the ideal candidate for the fretsaw, since there is only a small number of veneers required, and the grain directions of the components are not complex (as might be the case in a marquetry picture). The use of a fretsaw is not only quicker, but also allows identical matched designs to be cut accurately, and all at the same time. Where the grain directions of pieces are complex, the need for careful positioning of each piece precludes this method.

Fig 10.21 This marquetry design is repeated on the same piece of work, making it an ideal candidate for the fretsaw. There are no complex grain configurations that would make using the fretsaw awkward.

PREPARING THE VENEER PACK

For cutting multiple pieces of a repeated design, the different species of veneer to be used in the marquetry panel are assembled as a pack, and the design is cut out with a fretsaw. Sheets of very thin ply or scrap veneer are placed as the top and bottom components (labelled A and E in Fig 10.22). The top piece carries the traced design and the bottom piece prevents any splintering out of the veneers that might otherwise be caused by the saw blade. (*See* Fig 10.23.) These two veneer pieces also provide some rigidity, and help to hold the veneers in very close contact with each other, to ensure accurate cutting.

The design can be either traced or glued onto the top piece. Cutting will destroy the original design if it is glued on, although a photocopy will overcome this problem, whereas tracing will allow the original design to be used again. It is a help, in assembling the veneers, to have a copy of the design to refer to. Note in Fig 10.23, that the pack is held together with small veneer pins driven through the edge that falls outside the drawn border. Alternatively, the pack could be secured with heavy duty staples.

Each layer of veneer in the pack becomes a jigsaw puzzle containing all the component shapes of the design. The design is completed by assembling the various parts from each layer.

Repeated designs can be created by including enough veneers in the pack to make up the pieces. For example, if a design demands three species of veneer, then by making up a pack in which the three veneers are repeated twice, you will create two similar designs. This is important in the

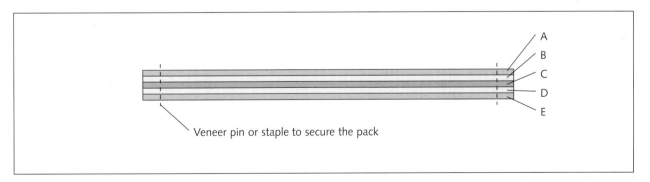

Veneer pin or staple to secure the pack

Fig 10.22 Making up the veneer pack. Components A and E are pieces of very thin birch ply or scrap veneer. Veneers B, C and D will form the marquetry design.

Fig 10.23 The veneer pack as it will look prior to cutting the design.

production of repetition work where two or more identical patterns are needed.

USING THE FRETSAW

Before describing the process of cutting a veneer panel with a fretsaw, let us look at how the tool should be used. The fretsaw should be held vertically and moved up and down with small strokes, and the veneer pack should be supported by a small marquetry table while you cut it. If the saw is off the vertical, the component veneers will not make good joints – the pieces will either be too small or too large because of the angle of cut. (*See* Fig 10.24.) Maintaining the fretsaw in the vertical position ensures that close joints will be made when the various components are reassembled.

The nature of fretsaw blades should also be considered. A saw blade will always produce a kerf, i.e. a gap caused by the removal of material by the blade. For this work, where close-fitting joints are essential, the blades need to be very fine. Blades

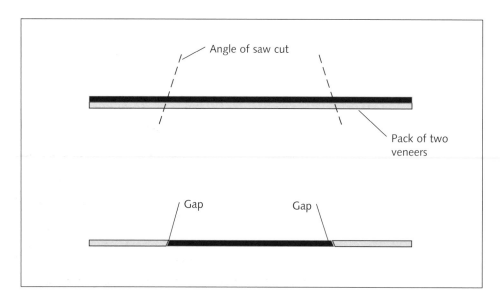

Angle of saw cut

Pack of two veneers

Gap   Gap

Fig 10.24 If the saw is used off the vertical, the component veneers will not make good joints – pieces will either be too small or too large because of the angle of the cut.

can be bought in a range of sizes: a grade 2/0 blade is fine enough for most purposes, with the finest available being a grade 6/0.

Blades can be bought for cutting either metal or wood: some marquetry work involves the use of metal inlays, and metal cutting blades are used for this.

There are two tooth configurations available, single and double (*see* Fig 10.25). The double-toothed blades allow easier clearance of the sawdust as they cut. The single-toothed blades are designed for general woodcutting. Most metal cutting blades are single-toothed, although there is also a spiral (helical) piercing saw blade for roughing out work in metal.

Fretsaw blades are fragile objects because of their fineness, and the finer they are, the greater the risk of them breaking. Because of this, the veneer pack is always moved gently into the blade, not the other way round, without pressure.

CUTTING OUT THE DESIGN

There is a necessary order to cutting out the design from the pack of veneers. The basic principle is to start from the inside of the design, and work towards the outside. If you start from the outside and work inwards, it will all fall apart! Thus, because the first cut must be near the centre of the design, you will need to drill a small hole at the point from which you will start cutting. Figure 10.26 shows a jewellers' piercing drill being used to pierce the veneer pack. Clearly, this hole should only be large enough to allow the blade to be passed through the pack before being secured in the saw frame (*see* Fig 10.27), so that no trace of its existence is left when the design is assembled and laid.

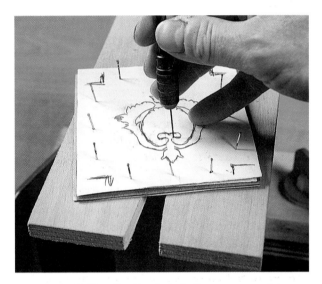

Fig 10.26 Making the tiny hole in the veneer pack to take the saw blade.

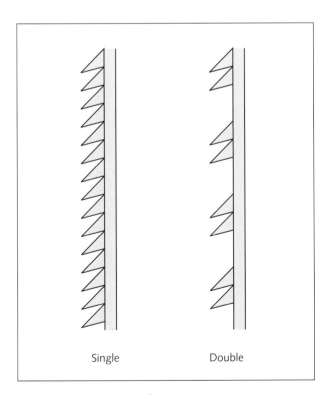

Single   Double

Fig 10.25 Saw tooth configuration.

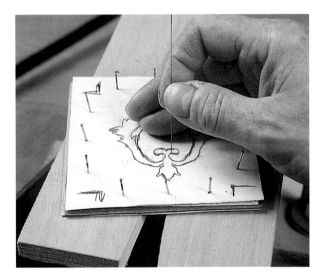

Fig 10.27 Threading the saw blade through the hole.

'WASTE' PIECES

After the various components of the design are cut out, the veneers are separated and assembled on a baseboard prior to laying. This will leave a number of pieces of veneer that do not form part of the original design. What of the remaining pieces? You will actually have two mirror image designs, as shown in Fig 10.28. When expensive species are used, this provides an opportunity to reduce wastage by incorporating the mirror image into another item. This was a common practice in days gone by. For example, Boulle work, in which brass was inlaid into tortoiseshell, was expensive, even by the standards of the late seventeenth and early eighteenth centuries when this method was common in pieces of high quality, so the remaining components were used in another item of furniture. In fact, there are quite a number of recorded examples of furniture whose surface decorations are a mirror image of each other.

ASSEMBLING THE COMPONENTS

Referring to the original drawing of your design will help you assemble the components, especially with fairly complex designs. In fact, it is a good idea to position the items on a photocopy of the original drawing as they are cut from the pack and separated from the unwanted pieces. This will help you keep track of them and avoid losing any. The problem, however, is that the completed design must then be moved to the groundwork for laying,

or stored away safely prior to this. For this, the veneers must be spot glued onto backing paper to hold the components together. How this is done depends on whether or not the design is symmetrical.

The backing paper will be glued onto the face side of the design, i.e. the side that will be the upper surface when it is laid. If the design is symmetrical, it will not matter which side of the veneer is glued to the paper, since the reverse side of the assembled pattern will be identical. (Figure 10.29 shows a symmetrical design.) However, an asymmetrical pattern, if turned over, will lead to a

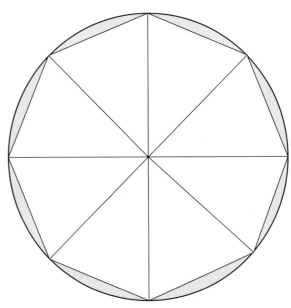

Fig 10.29 This symmetrical pattern will look the same whichever face is laid on the groundwork.

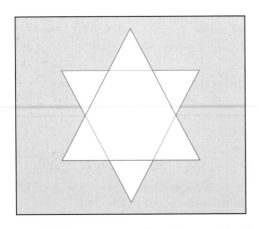

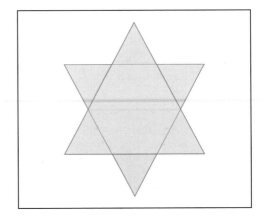

Fig 10.28 A pack of two veneers will produce two identical images, but with colour reversal.

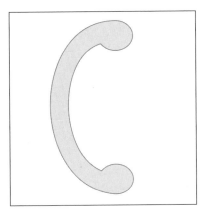

Fig 10.30 An asymmetrical design like this 'C' scroll can only be laid on one side.

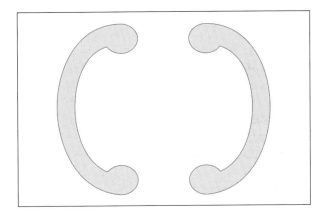

Fig 10.31 Two asymmetrical designs can be used to create a symmetrical pattern in the overall work.

mirror image of the original shapes (*see* Fig 10.30), so the side that is known to be the face side must be the one that is glued down. Identical asymmetrical designs can be used to create a symmetrical pattern, by gluing the designs to the paper on opposite faces (*see* Fig 10.31).

After gluing to the backing paper, store the panel under some pressure to maintain flatness.

The glue used for this task must be reversible, to allow for the paper to be removed after the marquetry panel has been laid. Spot gluing with animal or PVA glue will allow easy removal of the paper later.

INCORPORATING A MARQUETRY PANEL

There are two methods for incorporating a marquetry panel into your work (*see* Fig 10.32). One is to use the panel as a template to mark its shape on the surface of the work, and then to cut away the marked area from the work, and insert the marquetry panel in the space produced. (Refer to Chapter 8, page 103, for more details of this approach.)

The second method is to include the background veneer in the pack to be sawn. This is impractical, however, if the total surface area is large. Furthermore, as the saw cuts through the veneer pack it creates a kerf, or very small gap, where wood is lost in the form of sawdust. To a large extent, this can be masked when reassembling the design afterwards, and this masking is further aided

by the swelling of the fibres during laying, because of the glue used.

However, the gap between the main design and the background is often more obvious than those within the design. Even though the saw blade is very thin, and does not create a very wide kerf, the impact is cumulative. In other words, if the design is complex, with more than several components, the overall amount of lost material can be difficult to hide.

Because of these problems, it is common for the main panel of a marquetry design to be made using the fretsaw method, with its final incorporation into the design achieved using a modification of the window method, i.e. by using the marquetry panel as a template.

THE MACHINE FRETSAW

The old-fashioned marquetry donkey was the forerunner to the machine fretsaw (*see* Chapter 1, page 5). They are not widely available now, although plans to make your own are quite readily available. Many commercial marquetry workers do possess marquetry donkeys.

The great advantage of the machine fretsaw is that it leaves both hands free to manipulate the veneer pack. Also, much has been made of keeping saw blades vertical and this is much easier to do by setting up a machine accurately.

For repetitive work involving the use of quite thick veneer packs to produce a number of identical designs, a machine makes the task a good deal easier for two reasons. The first is that it takes the effort out of the job of cutting through a thick veneer pack, and the second is that it makes it easier to maintain the accurate angle for the blade.

The ease with which an electric machine cuts the veneer can lead to over-cutting the outline, so remain on your guard. It is important to remember not to push the pack into the blade to force the cut: it is inevitable that the blade will break if you attempt this.

ADDING A BORDER AND LAYING

The method of adding a border, and string if required, is not significantly different from that adopted for other veneering techniques. If you do intend to add a border, then it is advisable to make the marquetry panel slightly larger all round to allow for trimming. This does not have to be a great deal – certainly no more than $^1/_8$in (3mm) on each side. It is very unlikely that you will be able to produce edges that are straight and even enough to

add a border directly. You will need to trim the edges straight first to even them up. This is very simply done with a knife and straightedge. For small panels this can be done without the aid of measuring up – simply trim the edges straight, removing the minimum amount required. However, for large work, or where the dimensions of the panel must be specifically adhered to, the panel could be placed onto a template marked with the panel boundaries, and the edges trimmed on the template, to the drawn lines.

Strings and borders can then be added as described in Chapters 6 and 8. What you do have to bear in mind is the care that must be exercised when handling the work. While PVA glue rubbed into the rear of the joints will hold them together very successfully, it should always be remembered that the complex design is made up of a large number of pieces. It should be treated as a fragile item and handled very carefully, without flexing. It is a good idea to keep the work on a good, flat baseboard and to transfer it to any template or eventual groundwork directly from this board.

Marquetry work can only be laid using one of the press methods described in Chapter 5.

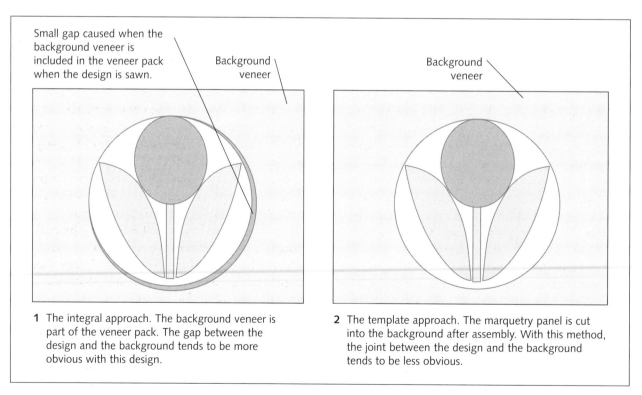

1 The integral approach. The background veneer is part of the veneer pack. The gap between the design and the background tends to be more obvious with this design.

2 The template approach. The marquetry panel is cut into the background after assembly. With this method, the joint between the design and the background tends to be less obvious.

Fig 10.32 The two approaches to incorporating a marquetry panel.

11

FINISHING AND POLISHING

♦ **THE FINISHING REGIME**

♦ **SMOOTHING THE WORK**

♦ **STAINING THE WORK**

♦ **POLISHING**

THE FINISHING REGIME

While there are certain differences in approach to finishing and polishing veneered work rather than solid wood, in most respects the materials and procedures are the same. Knife-cut veneers, being very thin, need to be treated very carefully when subjected to the use of abrasive paper: it does not take much to cut right through to the groundwork. Also, the method of producing these veneers tends to make them more porous than the solid wood equivalent and it may be necessary to use a grain filler to fill up these pores (*see* page 140). A veneered surface may take on a slightly deeper colour than the solid wood, and this should be borne in mind if you are mixing veneered and solid wood components in any work. On the plus side, the veneer surface will be free of the blemishes that are common to solid wood, such as torn-out grain and general unevenness. However, the main difference in the approach to finishing veneered

work as opposed to solid wood is in the initial preparation for smoothing the surface. Materials for smoothing a veneered surface are confined to the finer grades of abrasive paper – no smoothing plane or coarse abrasive paper.

The type of finish you apply is a matter of personal preference at the end of the day, but there are clear advantages and disadvantages to using particular finishing techniques. Of course, it is not mandatory to apply any finish, but it does help to protect the work and can also produce interesting optical effects in figure and colour contrasts.

For many woodworkers, the finishing process is fraught with anxiety – what to do, with what and when? There is a worry that this final stage may, somehow, ruin all the hours of work that have been put in. I am asked more questions about this aspect of working with wood than any other. The reason, I guess, lies in the very confusing array of finishing products on the market and the claims made for them in terms of physical properties and appropriate applications. Then there is the difficulty of compatibility: is it all right to use X with Y?

Achieving a good finish is a matter of matching the finishing requirements with the properties of the various finishes available, and following the correct order of procedures, as listed below:

- Smooth the veneered surface.
- Stain if this is appropriate (marquetry, parquetry and inlaid work are not usually stained as this would destroy the colour contrasts).
- Fill the grain if required.
- Polish.

SMOOTHING THE WORK

You need to remember that veneers are pretty thin and that there is a limit to the amount of sanding that can be done. If care is not exercised, disaster will be waiting around the corner.

Another potential difficulty arises from the varying grain directions that are often a feature of veneered work. It is good practice to sand the work along the general direction of the grain, but where grain direction is varied, this is not always possible. Figure 11.1 shows the general direction of sanding for different veneering patterns. The main point to remember is that the direction of sanding should, as far as it is possible, be in the general direction of the grain.

A third difficulty may arise as a result of contamination of lighter coloured veneers by sanding dust from darker ones. Under no circumstances must there be any contact with moisture as this would drive the coloured dust into the light veneer. The best approach is to use a dusting brush or, better still, an air jet from a small compressor, to clear the work of dust. Any hard rubbing will simply ingrain the contamination.

For smoothing veneer, the finer grades of paper must be used (e.g. 240 grit). An orbital sander is fine on flat areas of single-species veneers, but where more than one species has been used, and particularly where there are large colour contrasts, hand sanding is advisable. On flat surfaces use a cork sanding block. On shaped work a sanding block with a profile that is the reverse of the work should be made (see Fig 11.2).

As light sanding progresses, the work should be regularly dusted. This is especially important with

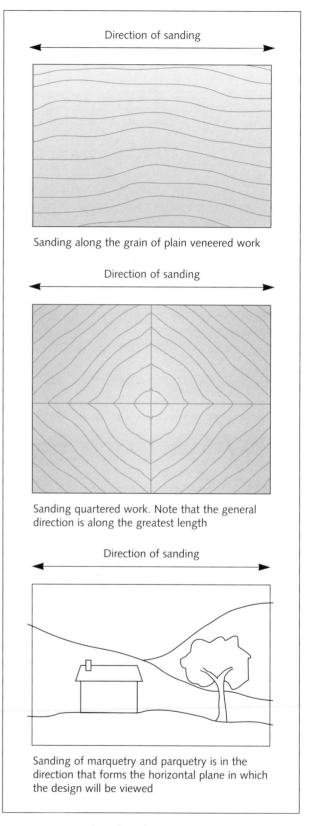

Sanding along the grain of plain veneered work

Sanding quartered work. Note that the general direction is along the greatest length

Sanding of marquetry and parquetry is in the direction that forms the horizontal plane in which the design will be viewed

11.1 Direction of sanding for veneers and marquetry panels.

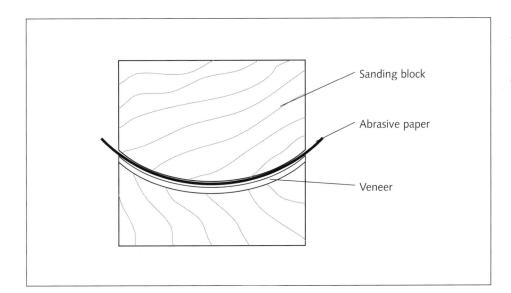

Fig 11.2 The use of a shaped sanding block for shaped work – the block has a reverse profile of the work.

Sanding block

Abrasive paper

Veneer

mixed-species work where continual sanding will itself cause darker dust to become irreversibly ingrained in lighter coloured species. Some readers may be familiar with the practice of wetting the surface to raise the grain after sanding, then sanding again once dry. Under no circumstances should this be done where mixed species have been used as any contaminating dust will be ingrained.

STAINING THE WORK

Staining veneers once they have been laid, where mixed species and colours are used, will prove to be problematic. Attempting to colour small areas will be very unsatisfactory, as no matter how much care is exercised there will almost certainly be a leaching of colour across veneer joints. The best advice for this sort of work is to stain before laying. For work that consists of a single species, staining can be carried out as though it were of solid wood. Chapter 4 describes the most common staining materials.

To stain a piece, pour the stain into a suitable wide container – not plastic if you are using a solvent-based stain, as it may dissolve the plastic! Make a pad of absorbent and lint-free fabric, dip this into the stain and allow it to soak up the liquid. Wear protective clothing, especially rubber gloves, and protect the surrounding area with paper or sheets. Gently squeeze the surplus stain out of the pad on the side of the container and then work the stain over the veneered surface with a circular motion to quickly cover it. The stain

should flow freely onto the surface, but should not form obvious puddles. If it doesn't flow, dip the pad again. Continue working until you are satisfied that the stain has penetrated the surface evenly. Finally, wipe the pad up and down the surface, in straight strokes along the grain, to even out the colour and remove any obvious circular path made by the pad. Allow the stain to dry overnight in a warm place.

FILLING THE GRAIN

As the manufacturing process of veneers sometimes makes them more porous than solid wood, if you want a perfectly smooth, glass-like finish, you will need to fill the pores of the wood first. This can be done in a number of different ways. Filling the grain is not obligatory, but it is the only satisfactory way of ensuring mirror finish, as exemplified by the surface of pianos. If you intend to use wax polish, grain filling has the distinct advantage of reducing the number of coats of wax needed to gain the desired effect. It also offers some protection against the penetration of dirt. Use a sanding sealer.

Sanding sealers and the main polish must be matched. In other words, the sanding sealer and the main polish should be essentially similar, and therefore compatible, materials. A shellac-based sealer should be used under french polish and wax polish and a catalysed sanding sealer should be used under catalysed lacquers. The best plan is to buy the sealer and main polish from the same source (see Suppliers on page 156).

APPLYING SEALER

Sealer is applied after the surface has been smoothed and stained (if a stain is used). The process of applying a grain-filling sealer is as follows.

1 Stir the sealer vigorously to ensure that any sediment is distributed throughout the liquid.

2 Apply the sealer evenly over the surface with a brush, along the grain, and force it well into the grain. Allow the sealer to dry and harden for the time specified by the manufacturer. This is important because the next stage will not be successful if the sealer is even slightly soft: the abrasive will only 'bite' the sealer if it has been allowed to harden thoroughly. Do not worry about the odd speck of dust or hair becoming trapped in the sealer. These will be sanded out later. However, at the same time, do not work in a very dusty atmosphere – that is a recipe for disaster because you will never achieve a flawless surface that way.

3 Using very fine abrasive paper, gently rub the surface smooth again. This is where you will notice something interesting. The abrasive paper will 'bite' the sealer and smooth it very quickly because of the powder it contains. A dust will build up quickly and you will need to dust the surface down quite regularly to examine the progress. When the surface is smooth, and all adhering dust and hair have been removed, give the work a final dust down ready for the top coats of polish.

The powder in the sealer has two purposes. First of all it gives the abrasive powder a bite, so it is more effective in smoothing the surface. Second, the powder enters the pores of the wood and helps to fill them. You may find that a second coat of sealer is necessary on very porous or open-grained veneers, for example, oak.

POLISHING

CHOOSING THE FINISH

There are a number of factors to be considered when deciding on an appropriate finish.

How much wear is the work likely to suffer? This is an extremely important consideration. Anything likely to be handled a great deal will become grubby very quickly. Cleaning will be virtually impossible if there is no finish to protect the work, but, on the other hand, any finish will have some effect on colour. Even the clearest and most colour-free polish will alter the colour of the work to some extent. At the very least it will enhance the dominant colour hue, and with all marquetry, parquetry and inlaid work, the contrast between veneer colours may be increased.

Are there colour contrasts that need to be preserved? The use of any coloured finish will reduce the impact of marquetry, parquetry and inlaid work. The finish for such work needs to be as colourless as possible to preserve the contrasts.

Is the veneered piece complete in itself or will it form part of a larger piece? Where a veneered piece does form part of a larger item, such as a table top, it is generally necessary to use the one finish for the whole item, so the requirements of all the timbers used must be taken into consideration.

In the case of restoration work, what was the original finish? The nature of the original finish must be taken into account. Old work is likely to have been french polished, and purists would be inclined to renew this rather than apply a more modern material such as polyurethane.

What quality finish do you want? Different finishes may give a high gloss film or a low 'natural' lustre: the quality that you want your work to have is a matter of personal preference. The most common polishing materials are:

- Wax
- French polish
- Polyurethane
- Cellulose or two-part catalysed lacquers.

WAX POLISH

The ease of application of wax polishes needs to be balanced against their general lack of durability.

Wax does provide some protection, but not against the effects of handling. However, it does give a wonderful low, natural lustre and, as such, is ideal for small items, like marquetry boxes and pictures, that will not be handled much. In fact, such items may suffer from the effect of a high lustre that could create distracting reflections.

As there are many good proprietary brands of wax polish available, it offers no advantage to make your own. Wax polish is available in two forms; either a solid wax paste or a cream. The creams are best used as a light dressing on work that has been varnished, french polished or lacquered, as the wax content is relatively low compared with the wax pastes. The high wax content of the pastes makes them ideal for unfinished work as they create a high build after only two or three coats. Even so, it is worth first giving the work a thin coat of pale french polish to partially seal the grain. This has two advantages: it provides some protection against the penetration of grime into the grain and the very act of adding an additional barrier reduces the amount of wax absorbed into the surface which, in turn, means that less polish is needed.

APPLICATION

If a coat of french polish has been used, allow a good few hours for it to harden thoroughly before waxing. Apply the wax polish with a lint-free cloth in small, circular paths, to rub it well into the surface. The amount applied should be generous, without leaving a heavy deposit behind – such a deposit will make the polish very much harder to burnish. Allow the wax to dry for a good hour before burnishing the surface with a clean cloth.

When the first coat is burnished, apply a second, lighter coat, leave for a further hour and burnish again. More coats can be applied in a similar manner, if required.

FRENCH POLISH

This is based on a solution of shellac in alcohol. It provides a fast-drying finish that lies as a hard film over the work, and forms a better protective finish than wax, though it is not resistant to heat, water or solvents and any lengthy exposure to these will result in damage.

When most people think of french polish it is as the so-called piano finish – a high mirror gloss. However, it is much more versatile than this and can be applied to create a range of finishes from very dull to very high gloss. The finish required depends very much on the nature of the work. In general, a marquetry picture will probably look better if the polish has a low lustre to avoid distracting reflections, but for veneered furniture, there are no hard and fast rules.

My earliest recollections of french polish are images of my grandfather crushing flakes of shellac, pouring them carefully into a large medicine bottle to half fill it, and then topping it up with methylated spirits. The smell of the spirit is still a strong memory. I guess that for many people over 'a certain age' there are similar images associated with this most prestigious of finishes, which may go some way to explaining why it has maintained its reputation. In truth, most of the modern, synthetic industrial finishes are mechanically superior in that they are harder and more resistant to damage, but french polish represents a tradition of craftsmanship that no other finish possesses. Like wax polish, you can make your own french polish, but there is no real advantage in doing so as proprietary brands are of very high quality and are readily available.

There are several colours of polish made from different natural colours of shellac.

Garnet polish. This, a rich chestnut brown, is the darkest. While ideal for dark surfaces, such as mahogany, rosewood and walnut, it is unsuitable for use on work where different coloured veneers have been used. The depth of colour will obscure the contrasts in mixed-species work.

Button polish. This is also quite dark, but less so than garnet. The colour is somewhat reminiscent of old walnut with its honey gold hue. Indeed, button polish is very good for work made from walnut or other species of similar colour.

White/Transparent polish. Bleached shellac is used to make white polish (which looks cream!). Its opaque, milky appearance is due to natural waxes that are found in the shellac. If many coats are used, white polish will create its own, slightly greyish colour cast. It is useful as a sealer, when combined with wax polishing (*see* page 138). If the wax is removed from shellac it will produce a clear, pale amber polish called transparent polish. Where the colour of the work needs to be retained, transparent polish can be used without causing any appreciable change: this makes it excellent for all mixed-species work.

It is not feasible to cover the entire subject of french polishing in a book of this nature, but the descriptions given here will help you to create a very good finish. It does require skill, but this can be acquired without too much difficulty. Equally important is the need for patience and a meticulous approach to detail and the order of processes. There are four main stages to french polishing: staining, grain filling, bodying, and spiriting.

Staining will usually only be required on single-species work, if at all. In marquetry and parquetry, veneers can be stained prior to laying.

French polishing should always be carried out in a warm, dry environment.

GRAIN FILLING

If a mirror finish is required, the grain must be filled to reduce its absorption rate. The easiest method is to use one of the so-called sanding sealers. A sanding sealer is a polish that contains a very fine powder and, because of this, it needs to be well agitated before use to disperse any sediment at the bottom of the container. For use under a french polish, a shellac-based sealer is required.

Sealers are well brushed out on the surface of the work, so as not to create any heavy build-up that will spoil the finish later, and left to dry out for an hour or so. The work should then be very lightly sanded (taking care not to cut through to the veneer) and the resulting dust wiped away.

Once this is done, apply a second coat and repeat the sanding after it has dried. Two coats should be enough to thoroughly fill the grain.

BODYING

This is the process of building up a deep body of polish to give the familiar gloss, once the surface has been sealed. Successive, thin layers of polish are applied with a tool whose association with the technique has taken on an almost mystical significance – the rubber.

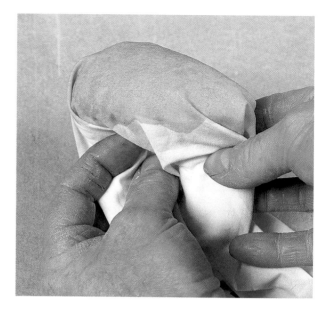

Fig 11.3 Making a french polish rubber.

A rubber is simply a pad of upholsterers' wadding enclosed in a rag (a piece of cotton cloth). The qualities of the rag are important to the finish of the polish: it must be very fine-grained and thin enough to allow a free flow of polish through it. An old cotton sheet or handkerchief are ideal, although I usually use plain cotton curtain lining. The shape of the rubber is also important as this will affect its handling. There should be a point at the front that will enable it to gain access to awkward corners and angles. (*See* Fig 11.3.)

A rubber is a prized possession if it is performing well, and they can be kept in service for a surprising length of time if properly looked after. If the rag becomes dirty and begins to inhibit the flow of polish through it, simply discard it and use a new cloth. The important thing is that the handling characteristics of the rubber (i.e. how it sits in the palm of the hand, the amount of polish it will hold, and its springiness) are too valuable to allow a good pad of wadding to be discarded until it is worn out! Whenever a rubber is not being used, it should be stored in a non-metallic, airtight container.

A new rubber is charged with french polish by removing the wadding and dipping it into the polish, which should be in a wide-necked container. Afterwards, squeeze out the surplus polish. This squeezing also helps to distribute the remaining polish evenly throughout the wadding. Reassemble the rubber – it is now conditioned and ready to use. As it dries out with use, it can be charged by removing the rag and dipping the face of the wadding into the polish. After replacing the rag, press the face against a piece of white paper to squeeze out the surplus polish and redistribute the rest.

While the actual technique of applying the polish is subject to some personal variation, there is a general pattern to the method. The principle is to apply very thin layers in such a way that any remaining open grain becomes filled and the polish film is burnished to a mirror-smooth finish. Polishing should always be carried out in a warm environment to prevent 'blooming' (the formation of a milky white cloud caused by moisture condensing and becoming trapped in the polish film).

SMALL FIGURES OF EIGHT

Applying the polish in small figures of eight, along the grain, helps to force it into any open grain that is remaining (*see* Fig 11.4). The amount of polish deposited as the rubber sweeps across the work can be quite critical. It is rather difficult to describe an amount. There should be an obvious wetness as the rubber passes over the work, but it should leave a fast-drying streak and there should be no pools or ridges. *The rubber must always be kept on the move.* If it is allowed to stop on the work there is a risk that it will adhere to it and spoil the surface. Adjust the pressure on the rubber to control the flow of polish. It will need to be increased as the rubber dries, and should then be recharged.

LARGE FIGURES OF EIGHT

No matter how carefully you apply the figures of eight, there will be evidence of this motion in the form of small, swirling tracks. These are eliminated by changing the motion to large figures of eight, continuing until the small tracks have been removed. All the while, because the general motion is at an angle to the grain direction, polish is being forced into the grain (*see* Fig 11.5).

STRAIGHT STROKES

Finally, the tracks caused by the large figures of eight are eliminated by applying the polish in straight strokes along the grain, carefully gliding the rubber off the work at the end of each stroke (*see* Fig 11.6).

The work should now be left for 15 minutes or so to allow the polish to dry sufficiently for you to apply another coat, using the same regime of figures of eight and straight strokes. You can apply as many coats as possible before the surface begins to resist by attempting to 'grab' the rubber because of its stickiness.

Allow the work to dry overnight. After it has had this time to dry, the film of polish will have shrunk a little and you may feel that more polish is needed. The process of bodying is repeated until you are satisfied with the outcome in terms of the depth of polish and the filling of grain.

You will then need to gently key the surface (which also removes any adhering particles of dust) by sanding with the very finest grade of abrasive paper you can find (say 600 grit wet-or-dry). It is

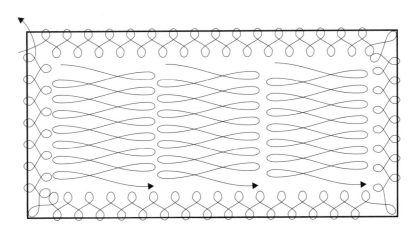

Fig 11.4 Small figures of eight.

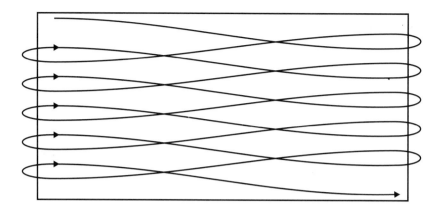

Fig 11.5 Large figures of eight.

Fig 11.6 Straight strokes.

important that there are no obvious scratches, just an overall dullness. You may feel that the finish you have achieved is very good and that there is no need to do anything else. However, to provide an extra special smoothness and lustre, the work can be finished off with thinned french polish in a process that is sometimes called spiriting and sometimes called stiffing.

SPIRITING (STIFFING)

The final stage of polishing is to apply very thin coats of polish that burnish the surface to a high gloss. Apply a body of thinned french polish (2 parts polish to 1 part alcohol or methylated spirit). This needs to be done very carefully as the spirit can be very fierce and pull up the film of polish! Allow the polish to dry for 15 minutes or so before repeating the process. After the second coat, the sheen should have returned. If it has not, apply a third coat.

What happens now has led to the process being given its very descriptive title. Subsequent coats should be as straight strokes along the grain. Leave at least 10–15 minutes between applications. As you continue working, the rubber will want to stick to the surface. This is good! The rubber is now doing its job of burnishing the surface to a high gloss. The paradox is, rather than speed up the movement over the surface (which will only result in tearing it up), you should slow down the movement. You may even need to increase the pressure slightly to maintain control of the rubber. Another important factor is to ensure that the strokes are dead straight along the grain. As you apply more layers, you may need to allow more time between coats. Ultimately, you will finish up with a mirror gloss, at which point stop and pack away the rubber until the next job. Allow the surface to dry and harden for a couple of days before putting the item into service.

POLYURETHANE VARNISH

As a hard-wearing, easy-to-apply finish, polyurethane takes some beating, although it does tend to suffer from a mixed reputation. While french polish carries a mystique and reputation for high quality, polyurethane has tended to represent the opposite end of the quality spectrum. Nothing could be further from the truth, though, because if care is taken in applying polyurethane, which comes in a range of lustres, it can look very good.

The problem with the finishes described so far is their general lack of durability. Wax needs continual maintenance, with an occasional re-application, and is not greatly resistant to moisture or heat. It will also become grubby if handled too much. French polish, on the other hand, has much greater mechanical strength. Even so, it is unsuitable for use on items that are likely to be in contact with hot cups, water (as with pot plants), or alcoholic drinks. Exposure to heat, water or alcohol may result in very severe damage. For items such as small occasional or coffee tables and trays, it is advisable to choose a finish that will be more durable – polyurethane varnish or a catalysed finish.

Varnishes have the advantages of having an uncomplicated application method, a high build, and a range of lustres (high gloss, semi-gloss or satin, and matt) and colours. All can be mixed to provide a customized colour and lustre.

APPLICATION

There is a point of view that varnish represents an inferior approach to wood finishing. I believe that this is really more to do with the way the varnish has been applied than with the nature of the material itself. There is no reason why a skilfully applied varnish cannot look as good as any other finish. The secret lies in the quality of the applicator and the skill with which it is used.

Varnishes are usually applied with a brush, but it is possible to use a rubber very similar to that used in french polishing.

BRUSH

The brush should be the best quality paint brush and must be reserved solely for varnishing. If it is used for painting, subsequent use for varnishing may result in contamination of the finish by flecks of paint or by clouding. Brush marks are considerably reduced or avoided by using 'laying off' strokes. These are very gentle strokes along the grain, using only the bristle tips, once the surface has been coated with varnish. (*See* Fig 11.7.)

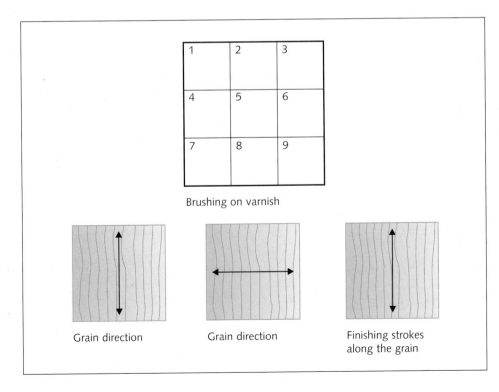

Brushing on varnish

Grain direction

Grain direction

Finishing strokes along the grain

Fig 11.7 Large areas are varnished one section at a time, with the final laying off strokes along the whole length of the work.

RUBBER

Make up a rubber (*see* Bodying under French Polish, on page 140). It needs to be generously filled with varnish by dipping. Varnish straight from the tin may be a little too viscous to apply successfully in this way so it may be better to thin it a little with paint thinners (white spirit), adding about 10% by volume. Rubbers are ideal for small items where it would be difficult to use a brush.

Use straight strokes along the general direction of the grain or, where this is not obvious, in the line of the longest length of the work. Because varnish is more sticky than french polish it does not have the same flow rate out of the rubber. It needs to be much wetter than a french polish rubber, and to be recharged very frequently. This process of polishing is very slow as several hours drying in a warm room are needed before another coat can be applied. (Store the rubber in a sealed container between coats.) Nevertheless, the method eliminates any tendency towards leaving brush marks. Apply as many coats as you need.

CATALYSED LACQUERS

The finishes so far described all have one feature in common: they harden through the process of solvent evaporation. Catalysed lacquers take this one stage further. After the initial drying period, a catalyst in the lacquer brings about a chemical reaction in the film that leads to further hardening through chemical change. This results in a polish that is highly resistant to mechanical damage, heat, water and other solvents.

Lacquers of this type are very fast-drying because they are based on highly volatile (and potentially dangerous) solvents, and are designed to be sprayed rather than applied by hand. However, there are brands of lacquer that are sold for the small user and formulated for brush application.

There are two forms of catalysed lacquer. The first, pre-catalysed lacquers, have the catalyst added during manufacture. Provided they are stored well-sealed, they have a fairly long shelf life. The second kind have the catalyst supplied separately, and are sold to the user as kits. The catalyst is added to the lacquer just before use: the proportion of catalyst (hardener) to lacquer varies between brands. Once the hardener has been

added, the shelf life of the prepared lacquer is relatively short and it must be used within the time period specified by the manufacturer. If unused lacquer is stored in an airtight container between coats, it could last a couple of days. The moral is, though, only mix enough for your immediate use.

What role can such lacquers play in veneered work? There are occasions where such lacquers are invaluable, for example, on coffee tables, and in car restoration, where veneered internal panels may need to be protected from humidity and rain – catalysed lacquers are perfect. However, you must remember to seal the back of the panel with the lacquer as well to prevent moisture penetrating from behind.

APPLICATION

These lacquers should be decanted into a glass or ceramic container for use as the catalyst could attack a metal container, and the solvent could dissolve a plastic one. Application by brush is more generous than with polyurethane because after initial solvent evaporation the real hardening process is a chemical one. The lacquer should be allowed to flow off the brush, but avoid runs and drips. Allow it to dry for the period recommended by the manufacturer before applying a second coat, not forgetting to use abrasives between coats to remove adhering dust particles and to smooth out any irregularities.

If required, the lacquer can be burnished to a mirror gloss, but you will need to ensure that the film of lacquer is deep and that no open grain is present. At least several days are allowed to pass after the last coat has been applied so that it is sufficiently hard, and the surface is thoroughly smoothed after this time with a very fine abrasive. Using a burnishing cream, often supplied with the lacquer, burnish the surface using a soft, lint-free cloth, with gentle pressure *along the length of the grain*. This last point is essential.

Brushes need to be cleaned immediately after use with the same solvent as the lacquer (a small amount is often supplied with the lacquer and it will pay you to buy a separate supply to allow for brush cleaning). If you leave the brush and the lacquer hardens, it may be impossible to clean afterwards, even if you use paint stripper.

RESTORATION AND WORKING WITH SAWN VENEERS

MISSING OR DAMAGED VENEER

All the techniques described in this book may be adapted to fit individual circumstances, and with restoration work this is often essential. Sometimes the work is straightforward, but on many occasions ingenuity and problem solving skills are demanded. The difficulty with much restoration is that it is not always possible to follow the same order of events and processes that make the task of building up any design so much easier. It is often necessary to work in a less than ideal way to achieve a satisfactory repair, simply because there is no other possibility.

Unprotected veneer edges are frequently damaged, although damage is by no means confined to this area alone. One very practical function of cross-banding at the edge of a panel is to provide some measure of protection for the main decorative veneer (*see* Chapter 6, page 74). Before the appearance of modern, synthetic glues, whose strength is, without question, far greater than any adhesive previously used, the edges of veneered work were especially vulnerable to damage. It was better to spoil a relatively narrow band of veneer at the edge rather than a highly figured, and relatively valuable veneer, so cheaper veneers were used in cross-banding, with the more valuable pieces kept for the less vulnerable main panels. If the edge veneer is straight-grained, with the grain direction running perpendicular to the edge, it is also much easier to effect an invisible repair.

DAMAGED CROSS-BANDING

Figure 12.1 shows damage to cross-banding that is fairly typical. The approach to this repair is to cut out the damaged area of cross-banding and replace it with sound veneer. By removing a section that is the entire width of the cross-banding, and cutting along the length of the grain, a good, invisible repair can be made.

REPAIRING CROSS-BANDING

1 Cut a strip of new cross-banding a little wider than the damaged area, to allow for trimming back. Use a straightedge to ensure that the two edges parallel to the grain are straight, and ensure that the edge that will butt up against the central panel does so accurately.

Fig 12.1 Typical damage to cross-banding.

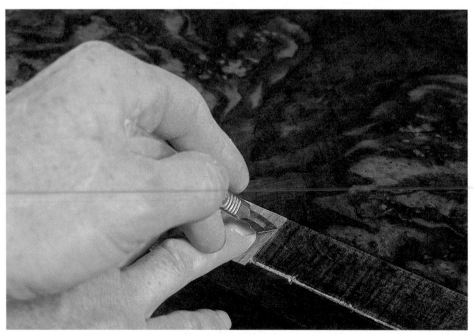

Fig 12.2 Mark the edges of the new veneer on the damaged section.

2 Position the patch over the damaged area and mark the edges on the veneer below with a veneer knife (*see* Fig 12.2).

3 Use a straightedge to cut through the damaged veneer, along the length of the grain, on the marked lines and remove the damaged cross-banding (*see* Fig 12.3).

This can sometimes be difficult, and there is always the danger of gouging the groundwork if you are not careful. On old pieces pearl glue will have been used and this can easily be softened with the application of heat. I frequently use the front tip of a warm clothes iron, or even a soldering iron if the area is small. Scrape away as much of the polish from the area as is feasible before pressing the warmed iron over the spot. As the glue softens, the veneer can be eased from the surface with a sharp chisel.

4 Clean the groundwork by scraping off the old glue with a small chisel or knife, then fit and glue the patch into place. It should fit perfectly, with the joints barely visible, if at all (*see* Fig 12.4).

Fig 12.3 The damaged veneer is removed and the area cleaned up.

Fig 12.4 The new patch in position.

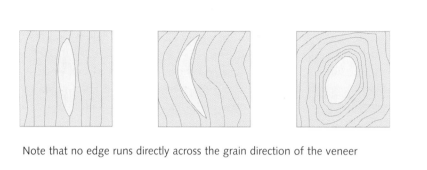

Fig 12.5 Suitable shapes for patching damaged veneers.

Note that no edge runs directly across the grain direction of the veneer

If you are using pearl glue, you may find it easier to spread a small amount of hot glue onto the patch rather than the exposed area of groundwork. Slide the patch into place, rub down with a small veneer hammer, and tape all the joints to minimize the risk of them opening as the glue dries.

If you are using PVA or some other resin glue, you will need to weight the patch in position. Remember to put a piece of paper between the patch and the weight to prevent surplus glue bonding the two together.

5 Once the glue has dried, trim the patch to remove the excess width, clean it up and then smooth, stain and polish as required (*see* Chapter 11). The finished patch will barely be noticeable.

GENERAL REPAIR OF MISSING OR DAMAGED VENEER

Damage may also occur in the centre of a veneer panel. The damaged area will need to be cut out and a patch fitted. Make the patch first, lay it over the damaged area, and score its outline on the surface. The damaged area is cut out and the patch glued into place following the same general method as for repairing cross-banding.

Careful matching of the figure and colour of the patch to the main veneer will help make the repair invisible. A square or rectangular patch will be very noticeable because at least two of the sides will cut right across the grain direction of the panel. The ideal is a shape whose sides follow the grain direction very closely (*see* Fig 12.5), but this is not always possible. The common feature of those shapes shown in Fig 12.5 is that the edges do not cut directly across the grain direction.

The edges of veneered boxes are especially vulnerable to damage (*see* Fig 12.6). Quite often the damage takes the form of a long strip that has broken off, or a corner that has been chipped away: both are quite straightforward to repair. The damaged area is cut back to create a good straight edge for the patch to butt up against. The patch may be triangular for corner chips, or may run parallel to the general grain direction for damage that runs the entire length of the veneer.

Fig 12.6 Common damage to the edges of boxes.

LIFTING VENEERS OFF THE GROUNDWORK

Frequently, extensive damage is caused by damp conditions, with very large areas lifting off the groundwork as the glue loses its hold: the tops of tables being damaged by vases of flowers is a typical problem. The damage was so bad that even the plywood groundwork was affected. For the purpose of illustration, the damaged area of veneer has been removed to expose the damage beneath. The first couple of layers of ply have separated, buckled and split. It is not possible to lay veneer over this area, so the groundwork has to be replaced.

The key question in such cases is: should time and effort be expended in saving as much of the original veneer as possible? My response to that question would depend on the relative value of the item (both in monetary and quality terms) and on its individual merits.

This example is not an old item and was picked up for £1 at auction because the damage was so extensive, but the walnut veneer has an attractive figure. Certainly, if this were an antique, I would not hesitate to save the undamaged veneer by lifting it off the groundwork. This is only feasible where water-soluble glues, which can be softened with the combined effort of heat and moisture, have been used. New furniture, for example, will have its veneers bonded to the groundwork with resin glues that are irreversible, so the following method of veneer removal will not work. In fact, it is unlikely that you will be able to remove in one piece, a veneer that has been bonded with resin glue.

Where water-soluble glues have been used and you wish to rescue as much of the original veneer as possible, either to re-lay it as part of the repair or, as I frequently do with highly decorative veneers, to store it for future repairs, the following method, which reverses the process of hammer veneering (*see* Chapter 5), is very effective.

REMOVING VENEER

1 Strip off any french polish or other surface finish to enable the moisture used in the softening process to penetrate the glue.

2 Soften the glue by placing a wet cloth over a small area near an edge of the veneer and running a hot clothes iron over the top. The steam this generates penetrates the veneer, softens its fibres to make it pliable, and liquefies the glue (*see* Fig 12.7).

Fig 12.7
Steaming veneer.

Fig 12.8 Lifting the steamed veneer with a metal spatula.

3 Ease the blade of a metal spatula under the edge of the veneer and gently separate it from the groundwork (*see* Fig 12.8). Remove the whole surface in one sheet by dividing the work into small areas and heating and lifting each area separately in this way.

4 After the sheet has been lifted it will be buckled and encrusted with dried glue on the underside. Clean off the glue, and then flatten the veneer using the method described on page 47.

Once removed, the veneer is ready for re-laying as if it were a new veneer, including jointing book-matched or quartered patterns. While it is possible to scrape off most of the old glue, you may need to remove the rest with a cloth moistened with hot water. You will need to clean off all the glue otherwise the veneer may not lie perfectly flat when it is re-laid.

One problem remains. It is inevitable that after trimming and jointing veneers as you re-lay them, the total area they cover will be smaller, and this may mean that the groundwork is left exposed around the edges. One way of overcoming this is to add a cross-banding if one was not present, or to renew any existing cross-banding so that the entire area is covered.

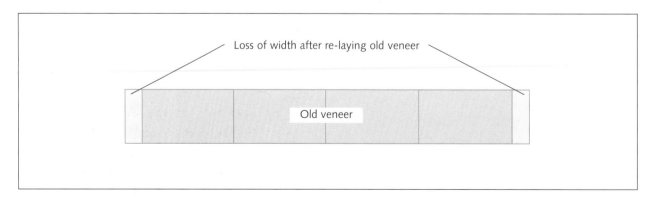

Loss of width after re-laying old veneer

Old veneer

Fig 12.9 There is a loss of width when jointed veneers are re-laid. The loss should be made up with new veneer.

An example of this problem that springs to mind is a job I had restoring an Edwardian upright piano on which the veneered lid had been badly damaged by long-term exposure to moisture. The veneer was a highly decorative burr walnut that would have been impossible to replace. I decided to lift the veneers and re-lay them. The lid was long and narrow, and the surface was veneered with a number of pieces joined to make up its length. In this case, there was no appreciable shrinkage in the width of the lid because of its narrowness, but as the veneers were laid and jointed, there was a considerable loss along the length of the lid (*see* Fig 12.9). This loss was made up with new burr walnut veneer. Overall, the original decorative effect was maintained so that the small piece of new veneer was not noticeable with a close inspection of the surface. The shortfall in width was about 4in (100mm) and in order to maintain symmetry, the shortfall was made good by adding an equal amount to both ends. The reasons for the loss of width are shrinkage that results from the process of lifting and, more importantly, because of the loss when the edges are trimmed during jointing.

VENEERS OF DIFFERENT THICKNESS

The basic process for repairing veneer is straightforward, but often the old veneer and the new patching veneer are of a different thickness. This can be a major barrier to effecting an invisible repair. It is worth making a dry-fit test before gluing so that you can take remedial steps if the veneers are of different thicknesses.

It is easier if the patch is slightly thicker and proud of the surface as it is a simple matter to level it after gluing into place. If the patch is thinner than the damaged veneer you can try laminating the patching veneer (*see* Chapter 2, page 12), but this does entail the risk of having to remove a good deal of the thickness to make it flush again. If you smooth through to the glue line, this cannot be easily disguised. My favourite method is to place a piece of thick paper or thin card beneath the patch to lift it up to the level of the original veneer. This paper should be glued into place before the veneer patch is fitted.

If the damaged veneer is very thick, it may be easier to make your own sawn veneer (*see* page 10).

REPAIRING BLISTERS

Blisters in old veneer are quite common: they are caused by the failure of the glue. This failure will almost certainly be the result of heat or water. Blisters cannot be flattened under the influence of heat because it will destroy the polished surface of the veneer. The best option is to split the bubble along the length of the grain (to make the split invisible), and insert glue under each side of the split as described in Chapter 5 (*see* page 73). Use a heavy weight to force the veneer down, first placing a sheet of paper over the bubble to prevent the veneer and the weight bonding.

REPLACING MISSING MARQUETRY AND PARQUETRY

It is particularly difficult to recreate the original design where the missing or damaged veneer is from marquetry or parquetry. With minor damage it is usually obvious what shape and species of veneer is required, but very large areas of damage, where the nature of the original design may not be obvious, present an ethical dilemma: should you recreate a design that you believe might have been there or should you leave the damaged area as it is? However, discussing the ethics of restoration is not the function of this book, so some practical advice on what to do here is more appropriate.

There are some questions I would ask before getting on with any repair work:

- What is the age and quality of the item to be repaired?
- Is the original design obvious from what is left intact?
- If the design is not obvious, do I have access to similar objects to obtain ideas of how the original design may have looked?

As a general rule of thumb, the original work and design should be restored, but this may require considerable knowledge about the nature of the piece and its history. Knowledge of the contemporary design and craftsmanship of the piece is the key to good restoration work, and you should not skimp on the research if you wish to be faithful to the design and period. A good example of this approach can be found in the revival of the Orient Express. A great deal of effort was put into tracking down original rolling stock and restoring the interiors. In one case, there were carriages whose Art Nouveau marquetry work had been badly damaged as a consequence of neglect. By a happy coincidence, the family-run firm that carried out the original work still existed. Not only that, they still had the original drawings and so were able to reconstruct the elaborate panels.

Such good fortune is pretty rare, of course, but the principle of researching how something should look is of great benefit. Of course, the item itself may be useful here. For example, it may be that the item for repair has several repeated marquetry panels, some of which may not be damaged, or where the damage is to a different part of the design. If it is not possible to copy the original design, because there are no other panels in the work, then you need to look at similar items to reconstruct a plausible design. In this, parquetry presents less of a difficulty than marquetry because of its repetitive design, and it can be a relatively easy process to reconstruct from even a fairly small area of original work.

When reconstructing large-scale damage, you should adopt the conventional techniques of marquetry and parquetry as described in Chapters 9 and 10, building the remaining work into the piece as part of the process. To do this, it may be easier to lift off what is left of the original veneers, place them on the templates you are using, and re-build the design around them.

REPLACING SMALL AREAS

Most restoration work on marquetry and parquetry involves the replacement of small areas and single pieces, and this is relatively easy to do. In effect, the gap left by the missing piece is a 'window' in the sense described in Chapter 10 (*see* page 121). The difficulty is that the outline cannot be scribed onto the replacement veneer in the same way. However, the shape and size will be obvious and

it can be copied using the technique of brass rubbing. To do this, place a piece of tracing paper over the area and use a pencil with a soft lead to 'rub' the outline. Glue the tracing onto the replacement veneer and cut out the shape using the sharp outline in the rubbing as the guide. The resulting piece of veneer should make a good fit. If it does not, don't accept a bad fit – repeat the rubbing and cutting until you do get a good one.

STAINING AND POLISHING VENEER PATCHES

In restoration it is necessary to colour and polish areas of patched veneer so that they match the surrounding area. It can be difficult to achieve a perfect match and some care is needed in smoothing the patch, selecting and applying a stain of the correct colour, and then building up the polish surface so that it is continuous with the original finish.

Begin by smoothing the patch with fine abrasive paper. Choosing the stain is the most difficult part of the process and involves some trial and error. For this you must test the stain on spare pieces of the veneer that was used for the patch. There are some important points to remember about this, too. The spare veneer must be sanded smooth and, very important, the side of the spare veneer used to test the stain must be the same as that of the patch itself. There is a very good reason for this – the grain orientation may be different on each side of the veneer and this can affect the final colour.

Test various stains on the patches (not forgetting to make a note of which is which). This alone will not necessarily be a perfect guide because the polish will also have an effect. You can simulate this effect by wetting the test areas to see how this changes the colour. When you are satisfied with the colour, stain the patch and, when it is dry, apply polish to the area with a small, soft-haired artists' brush. Allow the polish to dry, then apply another coat. Repeat the process until the level of the polish film is continuous with the surrounding area. In the case of wax polish, simply apply with a lint-free cloth. If you have used french polish, the whole work can be finished with a rubber to even out the surface.

WORKING WITH SAWN VENEERS

The veneer knife is only effective with thin, knife-cut veneers. While these are universally available today, and most modern pieces are made using them, sawn veneers are usually involved when restoring or making copies of antiques. Successful restoration work may dictate that a thick, sawn veneer be used for a repair, and these can be up to ⅛in (3mm) thick. The veneer knife cannot work effectively with these, and while all the techniques described in this book can be applied to sawn veneers, the cutting methods need to be adapted by substituting a veneer saw where a knife is specified.

Our forebears, who designed and executed intarsia and other inlay work, cut out the recess for the inlay with a rather lethal tool called a shoulder knife. This was, essentially, a knife blade secured to a long handle, the end of which rested on the craftsman's shoulder so that great pressure could be brought to bear on the wood. This must have been a pretty arduous task.

Another feature of sawn veneers, especially those that you make yourself, is that their thickness may be variable. However, this is not a problem as their extra thickness allows the use of a smoothing plane, and these can be used to level the work after the veneer has been laid.

PREPARING THE VENEER

Veneer straight from the saw is rough on both sides, and it is necessary to even out the side that will be glued to the groundwork to ensure good bonding. This can be done using a toothing plane in the same way as you would prepare a solid wood groundwork. (*See* Chapter 5, page 50.)

Secure the veneer to a work surface and then run the plane over it using a random pattern of passes over the entire surface. The important thing to remember is not to dwell on any one area for fear of hollowing it, but to make each pass cover the entire surface. Stop when the entire surface is covered with the tiny grooves caused by the plane iron. At this point, all high and low spots will have been eliminated.

You will almost certainly be using a solid wood groundwork in the case of restoration – remember to key its surface with the toothing plane as well.

An alternative to the toothing plane is a sanding linisher (*see* Fig 12.10), although care must be taken when using this tool as its action can be severe.

Fig 12.10 Smoothing the under surface of a sawn veneer with a linisher.

CUTTING AND SHAPING SAWN VENEERS

The veneer saw comes into its own with sawn veneers – a veneer knife cannot cope with their thickness. The curved edge to the blade prevents it snagging as it cuts. Figure 12.11 shows the saw being used against a straightedge. It is best operated by drawing the blade back towards you, rather than trying to use the conventional push pull action of saws, as this makes it much less likely to snag. Jointing edges should always be planed on the shooting board as you will not achieve even a reasonably close fit straight from the saw.

Since the veneer knife is not effective with these thicker veneers, some of the techniques described earlier in the book are not practicable. For example, all joints will have to be pre-cut and fitted prior to laying, including cross-banding joints and corner mitres. Parquetry and marquetry also require some adapting. In the case of parquetry, it is easier to cut the individual component shapes and fit them together rather than making up composite strips as described in Chapter 9 (see pages 106–109).

The accurate cutting of angles is a little more difficult with sawn veneers, but I find that a mitre saw does the job pretty well (see Fig 12.12). Cutting the parallel strips in the first place uses the same method as for cutting strips of knife-cut veneer. These can be prepared on the cutting jig using the spacers, straightedge and veneer saw. Shoot the edge that will be held against the side of the mitre saw before cutting the squares or diamonds. (See Chapter 9, page 107.) Each square or diamond needs to be fitted to its neighbours to build up the design. Clearly, there is ample opportunity for inaccuracies to occur. Shave each edge on the shooting board, taking off a whisker of wood, and start fitting them together. As you fit and tape the joints (see Chapter 5, pages 61 and 66), you may find that some additional trimming is necessary to keep the growing shape uniform.

In the case of marquetry, the fretsaw provides the only effective means of cutting the shapes. The window method must be adapted slightly for complex designs so that, after marking the outline of the window with a knife, the fretsaw is used to carefully cut around the outline (see Chapter 10,

Fig 12.11 A veneer saw and straightedge used to cut the veneer.

Fig 12.12 Using a mitre saw to cut diamonds. Note the use of a stop clamped to the cutting table to ensure that a constant length of veneer is achieved.

page 130). It is absolutely essential to keep the blade working vertically to obtain a good joint and to sand off any ragged fibres on the undersurface before fitting.

For simpler designs, make up a veneer pack as described in Chapter 10 (*see* page 129) and use the fretsaw as for knife-cut veneers. The pack will be thicker than usual, making it more difficult to obtain well-fitting joints, but, to quote a well-worn cliché, practice does make perfect.

Laying sawn veneers can only be done using some form of press: you cannot effectively hammer veneer with sawn veneers, especially where there are joints. (*See* Chapter 5.)

SUPPLIERS

The materials, tools and equipment mentioned in this book can be obtained from the following suppliers. Readers not living in the UK, please consult your local telephone directory or any of the magazines available on the subject, to locate stockists and suppliers.

VENEER

Many of these suppliers also sell other materials and tools that are associated with veneering, including stains and polishes.

ABBEY MARQUETRY
Unit 3 Furzewood House
Cranbourne Industrial Estate
Potters Bar
Hertfordshire
EN6 3JN

J. CRISPEN & SONS
92/96 Curtain Road
Shoreditch
London
EC2A 3AA

ART VENEER CO. LTD
Chiswick Avenue Industrial
    Estate
Mildenhall
Suffolk
IP28 7AY

C. B. VENEERS LTD
Progress Road
Sands Industrial Estate
High Wycombe
Buckinghamshire
HP11 4JD

**R. AARONSON (VENEERS)
LTD**
45 Redchurch Street
London
E2 7DJ

DESIGNER MARQUETRY
125a Bevan Street East
Lowestoft
Suffolk
NR32 2AQ

STAINS, POLISHES AND OTHER MATERIALS

**AXMINSTER POWER TOOL
CENTRE**
Chard Street
Axminster
Devon
EX13 5DZ

FIDDES & SON LTD
Trade Street
Cardiff
CF1 7TX

HOUSE OF HARBRU
Unit 3 Cuba Industrial Estate
Bolton Road North
Stubbins
Ramsbottom
Greater Manchester
BL0 0NE

LIBERON WAXES
Mountfield Industrial Estate
Learoyd Road
New Romney
Kent
TN28 8XU

W. S. JENKINS
Jeco Works
Tariff Road
Tottenham
London
N17 0EN

RUSTINS LTD
Waterloo Road
Cricklewood
London
NW2 7TX

JOHN MYLAND LTD
80 Norwood High Street
London
SE27 9NW

This list of suppliers is not exhaustive, but it will provide the core of a list to which you may wish to add further names. In addition to these suppliers, those readers whose interest in marquetry has been kindled may wish to know that there is a specialist society whose aim is to promote the craft. This organization is:

THE MARQUETRY SOCIETY
18 Blackthorn Grove
Bexley Heath
Kent
DA7 4EH

METRIC CONVERSION TABLE

INCHES TO MILLIMETRES AND CENTIMETRES

in	mm	cm	in	cm	in	cm
$^1/_8$	3	0.3	9	22.9	30	76.2
$^1/_4$	6	0.6	10	25.4	31	78.7
$^3/_8$	10	1.0	11	27.9	32	81.3
$^1/_2$	13	1.3	12	30.5	33	83.8
$^5/_8$	16	1.6	13	33.0	34	86.4
$^3/_4$	19	1.9	14	35.6	35	88.9
$^7/_8$	22	2.2	15	38.1	36	91.4
1	25	2.5	16	40.6	37	94.0
$1^1/_4$	32	3.2	17	43.2	38	96.5
$1^1/_2$	38	3.8	18	45.7	39	99.1
$1^3/_4$	44	4.4	19	48.3	40	101.6
2	51	5.1	20	50.8	41	104.1
$2^1/_2$	64	6.4	21	53.3	42	106.7
3	76	7.6	22	55.9	43	109.2
$3^1/_2$	89	8.9	23	58.4	44	111.8
4	102	10.2	24	61.0	45	114.3
$4^1/_2$	114	11.4	25	63.5	46	116.8
5	127	12.7	26	66.0	47	119.4
6	152	15.2	27	68.6	48	121.9
7	178	17.8	28	71.1	49	124.5
8	203	20.3	29	73.7	50	127.0

ABOUT THE AUTHOR

Ian Hosker began learning his craft at the age of 14 from his grandfather, whose range of skills seemed at the time to be awesome. What was at first natural adolescent curiousity became something of a passion as interest and skill grew – a phenomenon that many workers in wood will be familiar with. The channel for this passion was a business in furniture restoration and cabinetmaking that ran alongside a career in mainstream education. His clients include interior designers (some with very distinguished clients themselves, offering the opportunity to work on some very fine pieces) as well as private commissions.

Now, living in Devon with his wife and two children, he writes, teaches and demonstrates extensively on the subject of furniture - its history, construction and repair – while at the same time fulfilling his fantasy as a salty sea-dog. Furniture, however, remains his all-abiding passion.

This is Ian's third book, following *Complete Woodfinishing* and *Woodfinishing Handbook*, also published by Guild of Master Craftsman Publications Ltd.

INDEX

TITLES AVAILABLE FROM
GMC PUBLICATIONS

◆ BOOKS ◆

WOODWORKING

40 More Woodworking Plans & Projects	*GMC Publications*
Bird Boxes and Feeders for the Garden	*Dave Mackenzie*
Complete Woodfinishing	*Ian Hosker*
Electric Woodwork	*Jeremy Broun*
Furniture & Cabinetmaking Projects	*GMC Publications*
Furniture Projects	*Rod Wales*
Furniture Restoration (Practical Crafts)	*Kevin Jan Bonner*
Furniture Restoration and Repair for Beginners	*Kevin Jan Bonner*
Green Woodwork	*Mike Abbott*
The Incredible Router	*Jeremy Broun*
Making & Modifying Woodworking Tools	*Jim Kingshott*
Making Chairs and Tables	*GMC Publications*
Making Fine Furniture	*Tom Darby*
Making Little Boxes from Wood	*John Bennett*
Making Shaker Furniture	*Barry Jackson*
Pine Furniture Projects for the Home	*Dave Mackenzie*
The Router and *Furniture & Cabinetmaking* Test Reports	*GMC Publications*
Sharpening Pocket Reference Book	*Jim Kingshott*
Sharpening: The Complete Guide	*Jim Kingshott*
Space-Saving Furniture Projects	*Dave Mackenzie*
Stickmaking: A Complete Course	*Andrew Jones & Clive George*
Veneering: A Complete Course	*Ian Hosker*
Woodfinishing Handbook (Practical Crafts)	*Ian Hosker*
Woodworking Plans and Projects	*GMC Publications*
The Workshop	*Jim Kingshott*

WOODTURNING

Adventures in Woodturning	*David Springett*
Bert Marsh: Woodturner	*Bert Marsh*
Bill Jones' Notes from the Turning Shop	*Bill Jones*
Bill Jones' Further Notes from the Turning Shop	*Bill Jones*
Colouring Techniques for Woodturners	*Jan Sanders*
The Craftsman Woodturner	*Peter Child*
Decorative Techniques for Woodturners	*Hilary Bowen*
Essential Tips for Woodturners	*GMC Publications*
Faceplate Turning	*GMC Publications*
Fun at the Lathe	*R.C. Bell*
Illustrated Woodturning Techniques	*John Hunnex*
Intermediate Woodturning Projects	*GMC Publications*
Keith Rowley's Woodturning Projects	*Keith Rowley*
Make Money from Woodturning	*Ann & Bob Phillips*
Multi-Centre Woodturning	*Ray Hopper*
Pleasure and Profit from Woodturning	*Reg Sherwin*
Practical Tips for Turners & Carvers	*GMC Publications*
Practical Tips for Woodturners	*GMC Publications*
Spindle Turning	*GMC Publications*
Turning Miniatures in Wood	*John Sainsbury*
Turning Wooden Toys	*Terry Lawrence*
Understanding Woodturning	*Ann & Bob Phillips*
Useful Techniques for Woodturners	*GMC Publications*
Useful Woodturning Projects	*GMC Publications*
Woodturning: A Foundation Course	*Keith Rowley*
Woodturning: A Source Book of Shapes	*John Hunnex*
Woodturning Jewellery	*Hilary Bowen*
Woodturning Masterclass	*Tony Boase*
Woodturning Techniques	*GMC Publications*
Woodturning Tools & Equipment Test Reports	*GMC Publications*
Woodturning Wizardry	*David Springett*

WOODCARVING

The Art of the Woodcarver	*GMC Publications*
Carving Birds & Beasts	*GMC Publications*
Carving on Turning	*Chris Pye*
Carving Realistic Birds	*David Tippey*
Decorative Woodcarving	*Jeremy Williams*
Essential Tips for Woodcarvers	*GMC Publications*
Essential Woodcarving Techniques	*Dick Onians*
Lettercarving in Wood: A Practical Course	*Chris Pye*
Practical Tips for Turners & Carvers	*GMC Publications*
Relief Carving in Wood: A Practical Introduction	*Chris Pye*
Understanding Woodcarving	*GMC Publications*
Understanding Woodcarving in the Round	*GMC Publications*
Useful Techniques for Woodcarvers	*GMC Publications*
Wildfowl Carving - Volume 1	*Jim Pearce*
Wildfowl Carving - Volume 2	*Jim Pearce*
The Woodcarvers	*GMC Publications*
Woodcarving: A Complete Course	*Ron Butterfield*
Woodcarving: A Foundation Course	*Zoë Gertner*
Woodcarving for Beginners	*GMC Publications*
Woodcarving Tools & Equipment Test Reports	*GMC Publications*
Woodcarving Tools, Materials & Equipment	*Chris Pye*

UPHOLSTERY

Seat Weaving (Practical Crafts)	*Ricky Holdstock*
Upholsterer's Pocket Reference Book	*David James*
Upholstery: A Complete Course	*David James*
Upholstery Restoration	*David James*
Upholstery Techniques & Projects	*David James*

TOYMAKING

Designing & Making Wooden Toys	*Terry Kelly*	Restoring Rocking Horses	*Clive Green & Anthony Dew*
Fun to Make Wooden Toys & Games	*Jeff & Jennie Loader*	Scrollsaw Toy Projects	*Ivor Carlyle*
Making Board, Peg & Dice Games	*Jeff & Jennie Loader*	Wooden Toy Projects	*GMC Publications*
Making Wooden Toys & Games	*Jeff & Jennie Loader*		

DOLLS' HOUSES AND MINIATURES

Architecture for Dolls' Houses	*Joyce Percival*	Making Period Dolls' House Accessories	*Andrea Barham*
Beginners' Guide to the Dolls' House Hobby	*Jean Nisbett*	Making Period Dolls' House Furniture	*Derek & Sheila Rowbottom*
The Complete Dolls' House Book	*Jean Nisbett*	Making Tudor Dolls' Houses	*Derek Rowbottom*
Dolls' House Accessories, Fixtures and Fittings	*Andrea Barham*	Making Unusual Miniatures	*Graham Spalding*
Dolls' House Bathrooms: Lots of Little Loos	*Patricia King*	Making Victorian Dolls' House Furniture	*Patricia King*
Easy to Make Dolls' House Accessories	*Andrea Barham*	Miniature Bobbin Lace	*Roz Snowden*
Make Your Own Dolls' House Furniture	*Maurice Harper*	Miniature Embroidery for the Victorian Dolls' House	*Pamela Warner*
Making Dolls' House Furniture	*Patricia King*	Miniature Needlepoint Carpets	*Janet Granger*
Making Georgian Dolls' Houses	*Derek Rowbottom*	The Secrets of the Dolls' House Makers	*Jean Nisbett*
Making Miniature Oriental Rugs & Carpets	*Meik & Ian McNaughton*		

CRAFTS

American Patchwork Designs in Needlepoint	*Melanie Tacon*	Embroidery Tips & Hints	*Harold Hayes*
A Beginners' Guide to Rubber Stamping	*Brenda Hunt*	An Introduction to Crewel Embroidery	*Mave Glenny*
Celtic Knotwork Designs	*Sheila Sturrock*	Making Character Bears	*Valerie Tyler*
Collage from Seeds, Leaves and Flowers	*Joan Carver*	Making Greetings Cards for Beginners	*Pat Sutherland*
Complete Pyrography	*Stephen Poole*	Making Knitwear Fit	*Pat Ashforth & Steve Plummer*
Creating Knitwear Designs	*Pat Ashforth & Steve Plummer*	Needlepoint: A Foundation Course	*Sandra Hardy*
Creative Embroidery Techniques Using		Pyrography Handbook (Practical Crafts)	*Stephen Poole*
Colour Through Gold	*Daphne J. Ashby & Jackie Woolsey*	Tassel Making for Beginners	*Enid Taylor*
Cross Stitch Kitchen Projects	*Janet Granger*	Tatting Collage	*Lindsay Rogers*
Cross Stitch on Colour	*Sheena Rogers*	Temari: A Traditional Japanese Embroidery Technique	*Margaret Ludlow*

THE HOME

Home Ownership: Buying and Maintaining	*Nicholas Snelling*	Security for the Householder: Fitting Locks and Other Devices	*E. Phillips*

◆ VIDEOS ◆

Drop-in and Pinstuffed Seats	*David James*	Twists and Advanced Turning	*Dennis White*
Stuffover Upholstery	*David James*	Sharpening the Professional Way	*Jim Kingshott*
Elliptical Turning	*David Springett*	Sharpening Turning & Carving Tools	*Jim Kingshott*
Woodturning Wizardry	*David Springett*	Bowl Turning	*John Jordan*
Turning Between Centres: The Basics	*Dennis White*	Hollow Turning	*John Jordan*
Turning Bowls	*Dennis White*	Woodturning: A Foundation Course	*Keith Rowley*
Boxes, Goblets and Screw Threads	*Dennis White*	Carving a Figure: The Female Form	*Ray Gonzalez*
Novelties and Projects	*Dennis White*	The Router: A Beginner's Guide	*Alan Goodsell*
Classic Profiles	*Dennis White*	The Scroll Saw: A Beginner's Guide	*John Burke*

◆ MAGAZINES ◆

Woodturning • Woodcarving • Furniture & Cabinetmaking • The Router
The Dolls' House Magazine • Creative Crafts for the Home • BusinessMatters

---

The above represents a full list of all titles currently published or scheduled to be published. All are available direct from the Publishers or through bookshops, newsagents and specialist retailers. To place an order, or to obtain a complete catalogue, contact:

GMC Publications, 166 High Street, Lewes, East Sussex BN7 1XU, United Kingdom
Tel: 01273 488005 Fax: 01273 478606

Orders by credit card are accepted